TRANSNATIONAL LIBRARY RELATIONS

CONCEPTS IN COMMUNICATION INFORMATICS & LIBRARIANSHIP (CICIL)

General Editor : **S.P. AGRAWAL**

CICIL - 1 Development of Library Services in India : Social Science Information — **S.P. Agrawal**

CICIL - 2 Development of Documentation in India : Social Science Information — **S.P. Agrawal**

CICIL - 3 Unesco and Social Sciences : Restrospect and Prospect — **S.P. Agrawal** and **J.C. Aggarwal**

CICIL - 4 INDIANA : A Bibliography of Bibliographical Sources — **M.K. Jain**

CICIL - 5 Dimensions of Library and Information Science : Papers contributed in honour of the 61st birthday celebrations of Prof. P.N. Kaula — **V. Venkatappaiah** (Ed.)

CICIL - 6 Book Numbers : Some Indian Methods — **M.P. Satija** and **S.P. Agrawal**

CICIL - 7 National Policy for University Libraries in India : Problems and Perspectives — **N.B. Inamdar** and **L.S. Ramaiah**

CICIL - 8 Media Utilisation for the Development of Women and Children — **B.S. Thakur** and **Binod C. Agrawal**

CICIL - 9 Terrorism : An annotated Bibliography — **Susheela Bhan**

CICIL - 10 Transnational Library Relations : The Indo-American Experience — **M.B. Konnur**

CICIL - 11 Geography of Marketing and Commercial Activities in India (Documentation on Research Information) — **R.S. Dixit**

CICIL - 12 Information India 1988 : Global View — **S.P. Agrawal** and **J.C. Aggarwal**

CICIL - 13 Development of Higher Education Through Television — **Binod C. Agrawal** (in press)

CICIL - 14 Children's Television in India — **Binod C. Agrawal** (in press)

CICIL - 15 Television for Rural Development — **B.S.S. Rao** (in press)

CICIL - 16 A Study of Factors Influencing TV Communication for Rural Development Through Community Viewing — **Raja Pokharapurkar** (in press)

CICIL - 17 Communication Revolution : A Study of Video Penetration (in 5 vols.) — **Binod C. Agrawal** (in press)

CICIL - 18 Professionals in Organisation : A Study of Trained Librarians in University, Public and Special Libraries — **P.K. Jauyaswal** (in press)

CICIL - 19 Literature Search — **K.A. Issac** (in press)

CICIL - 20 Child Education in India : — **S.P. Agrawal** and **J.C. Aggrawal**

CICIL - 21 Lok Sabha Election Index to Scholarly Writings in Indian Educational Journals and Newspapers Since Independence India 1989 : A Study — **J.C. Aggarwal** and **S.P. Agrawal** (in press)

CICIL - 22 Islamic Studies in India — **Mohamed Taher** (in press)

CICIL - 23 Cultural Adaptation of Television and Video in Urban Millieu : A Case Study — **H.R. Trivedi** (in press)

Concepts in Communication
Informatics & Librarianship - 10

General Editor: **S. P. Agrawal**

TRANSNATIONAL LIBRARY RELATIONS
The Indo-American Experience

M. B. KONNUR

CONCEPT PUBLISHING COMPANY, NEW DELHI-110059
(INDIA)

ISBN 81-7022-260-5

First Published 1990

Madhukar Bhimrao **Konnur** (*b.* 1938)

Published by
Ashok Kumar Mittal
Concept Publishing Company
A/15-16, Commercial Block, Mohan Garden
NEW DELHI-110059 (India)

Lasertypeset by
Microtech Advance Printing Systems (Pvt.) Ltd.
H - 13, Bali Nagar,
NEW DELHI - 110015.

Printed in India by
Taj Press
DELHI-110006

To

SUJATA

for her gracious forbearance
during the long hours of study
and the writing which followed

FOREWORD

International programmes of cultural relations are carried on through both official and unofficial agencies. Cultural cooperation with other countries as an official government programme was inaugurated by the United States in 1938. At President Roosevelt's suggestion a significant step was taken in that year – a Division of Cultural Relations was created within the Department of State, for the purpose of "encouraging and strengthening cultural relations and intellectual cooperation between United States and other countries."

We librarians have been in the business of international cultural relations ever since Callimachus (*ca.*310 - *ca.* 240) of Cyrene went to Alexandria to build the famous library's collection and produced his 120-volume catalogue of the holdings in Greek literature.

"Transnational Library Relations: Indo-American Experience" by Dr. M.B. Konnur narrates the story of Indo-American cultural relations in the Library and Information Science field in its various facets for over seven decades.

The story begins in 1910. Baroda State, in western India, had a reputation for being progressive in many fields not the least in education and social reform. The then Maharaja of Baroda invited William Alanson Borden, an American professional librarian, to assist in the establishment of a complete modern library system in the State. Borden accepted the invitation, and within three years as Director of Libraries, he successfully completed his assignment – a network of free state aided libraries and reading rooms in all parts of the state and an agency for providing visual instruction for illiterates. He started a library school and a professional journal – *The Baroda Miscellany.*

Five years later another American was invited by the Punjab University for reorganizing the University library. He stayed only for one year – completed the reorganisation of the library, started a library school, brought out a Library Primer and submitted a "Report on Work in the Punjab University Library, Lahore." This report is listed in a recent publication – *Information Services in Muslim Countries: An*

Annotated Bibliography of Expert Studies and Reports on Library, Information and Archival Services, by Mumtaz A. Anwar (Mansell, 1985).

After India gained independence and especially during 1950's and 1960's American library specialists came to India in various capacities. Dr. Konnur attempts to investigate how and to what extent the services of library specialists on assignment in India assisted various institutions and attempts to measure their impact on library science education. He also provides useful data of financial aid received under various schemes and endeavours to evaluate their contribution to the enrichment of library collections in various institutions.

One of the cultural activities carried out by Governments commonly includes the establishment and support of cultural centres or institutes. The author presents a study of the activities and contribution of the USIS libraries in India, of the American Studies Research Centre and the American Institute of Indian Studies.

Finally the author attempts to assess objectively the Indian contribution to American librarianship. In the realm of cultural exchange there cannot always be a "reciprocity". Ideas can be revived and given a new life. So Ranganathan's ideas on the various facets of librarianship are our main coutributions not only to American librarianship but to world librardianship.

Dr. Konnur's book is a pioneering work and makes an important contribution on Indo-American cultural cooperation in librarianship and to comparative librarianship. We look forward to supplementary studies of indepth assessment of the impact of the wide range of cooperation for over seven decades.

B. ANDERSON

GENERAL EDITOR'S INTRODUCTION

Justice Mahadeo Govind Ranade once described India's connection with Great Britain as 'Divine dispensation' whatever that be, we could as well describ our relations with the nation halfway across the world – the USA – in somewhat similar terms.

In the following pages, Dr. M. B. Konnur delves into the history of one facet of these relations, namely, the field of Library and Information Science.

Dr. Konnur has made studious efforts to document the U.S. expertise and the financial aid that made the day for the library world here in India, and the singular contribution of Dr. S. R. Ranganathan in the evolution of thought processes in the U.S.

Have we profited to the maximum, progressed enough from this give and take ? Well, that is a different story altogether.

Meanwhile, we can express happiness at the fortuitous coincidence that the subscription libraries of the British Council and the entirely free libraries run by the U.S. Government continue to render excellent service to the reading public in India.

S. P. AGRAWAL

CONTENTS

LIST OF TABLES

ACKNOWLEDGMENTS

I would like to express my warmest appreciation to all those who helped in the preparation of this book, especially to M. R. Riswadkar, formerly Reader in Library and Information Science, University of Poona, who proved himself a scholar and without whose guidance I could not have completed my research; P. K. Garde, formerly Chief, Reader Services Division, Dag Hammarskjold Library, United Nations, for his inspiring, painstaking and intellectual guidance, accessibility, and warm encouragement at all stages in the preparation of this manuscript; B. Anderson, formerly Librarian and Head of Library Science Department, University of Bombay, for originally pointing the way to the subject of my study and also for kindly giving his consent to write an introduction to this book.

It is a common experience of many a research worker to find that he has only scratched the surface of the chosen problem and however creative and original he desires to be, many of his ideas and insights have come from stimulating associates. I am thus indebted to a large number of friends and colleagues, not only from India, but also from abroad, who have helped me at different stages in my research work. Their number is legion and I hope no one will feel slighted by the physical impossibility of listing all of them. However, my grateful thanks are due to:

Lester Asheim, Laurence J. Kipp, F. W. Lancaster, Maureen L. P. Patterson, Patrick R. Penland, Joseph Rosenthal and Ravindra Nath Sharma from the U.S. ;

George Chandler from Australia and Anis Khurshid from Pakistan;

Ganesh Bhattacharyya, Kalpana Dasgupta, K. S. Deshpande, K. S. Hingwe, N. B. Inamdar, V. A. Kamath, P. N. Kaula, P. S. G. Kumar, S. G. Mahajan, P. B. Mangla and A. C. Tikekar from India;

Daniel J. Boorstin, former Librarian, Library of Congress, for making certain documents available;

B. S. Kesavan for sparing some of his precious time to discuss certain points in my work;

R. Thiagarajan, Joint Adviser, Department of Science and Technology, Government of India, New Delhi, for his extensive interview;

Sharada Nayak (Director, USEFI, New Delhi), Joginder Singh, Heera Kapasi, R. Sathyamurthy, M. S. Shetge, Vera Kothavala, R. Thiruvengadam and Indira Soman (all from American Center libraries in India), Pradeep Mehendiratta, Shubha Chaudhuri and M. D. Bhandare (all from American Institute of Indian Studies), and Sreenidhi Iyengar of American Studies Research Centre, Hyderabad, for their help in my work;

Michael B. Pipkin, Donald C. Hausrath, E. Gene Smith and John C. Crawford for their cooperation in the present work;

Asia Foundation, Carnegie Corporation, Rockefeller Foundation and Unesco for providing certain documents required in the present work, as well as several universities and research institutions in India for making library facilities available to me;

University Grants Commission and Indian Council of Social Science Research (particularly S. P. Agrawal and S. D. Karnik) for their financial assistance to undertake travel in the country for data collection;

S. P. Agrawal, General Editor, CICIL, New Delhi, for inclusion of this work in the Series and M/s Concept Publishing Company, New Delhi, for undertaking the publishing of this book; and

The authorities of the University of Poona for granting me permission to publish my doctoral work.

M. B. KONNUR

1

INTRODUCTION

1. INTRODUCTION

It is patently unnecessary for the purpose of the present study to delve into a sweeping history of the origin and development of libraries. Nevertheless, the two countries whose mutual relations in the area of libraries and librarianship are considered here are so diverse in their antecedents that a brief sketch of the emergence of libraries in either of them does seem necessary as providing a perspective to more recent events.

2. HISTORY OF LIBRARIES IN INDIA

The history of India goes back to immemorial antiquity. However, several centuries had to elapse before ancient lore and learning were committed to writing since all knowledge in the ancient period passed from mouth to mouth and was transmitted from one generation to another by the aid of memory.[1] *Pandits* (scholars) in those days were, in fact, themselves living libraries. Naturally, "so long as there was reliance on memory alone, there was no library, indeed there could be none".[2] However, according to accounts provided by Agrawal, Chakravorti, Raghunandan Shastri, Chakravarty, Khurshid, and Inamdar and Riswadkar, excepting for a limited period in the entire history of Indian civilization, libraries in some form or other, did exist in India in very old times.[3-8]

Indians attached great importance to the maintenance of libraries, such as they were, and much emphasis was laid on the making of manuscripts over to the temple *bhandaras* (library collections in temples). Concomitantly with the spread of liberal education, all available manuscripts and other graphic materials were procured for use in almost all seats of learning, particularly in the universities at Nalanda, Taxila, Kanchi, Vikramasila and Varanasi. During his travel through the country, Hiuen Tsang broke his journey at several monasteries which, as seats of learning, were famous for their libraries and rare books. The most prominent libraries visited by him were those of the universities of Nalanda and Vikramasila, "the details of which we learn also from the accounts of the other Chinese pilgrim I-Tsing and from the Tibetan and Muslim sources as well".[9] Later, this library tradition continued to grow when Muslim power in India opened up new centres of learning and scholarship. But, with the decline of the Mughal empire, popular education received a setback. Consequently, ancient libraries were either destroyed or their collections were taken out of the country.

3. HISTORY OF LIBRARIES IN THE UNITED STATES

Compared to India, the United States (U.S.) is quite a young country. Its ascertainable history, by all accounts, goes back to only 500 years when the Europeans discovered that continent in 1492. Libraries in the U.S. did not, therefore, have to pass through the phases preceding the use of paper and print which libraries in ancient India had to, and library movement in that country may be thus said to have got a head start. The story of the spread of libraries in the newly-discovered country has been chronicled by some of the most eminent amongst American librarians. To begin with, there is Shera's paper which provides a brief account of the major phases of American library histography during the past one hundred and fifty years.[10] Sister O'Loughlin's study reveals influences evident in 1876 in the emergence of American librarianship;[11] and papers by Colson, Bryant, Vosper and Liebaers deal with other significant aspects in the rapid growth of libraries in the U.S.[12-15]

It can be seen from these writings that as a new nation on a new continent began to grow and develop, library movement too began to have its stirrings. Its origin, though, can be traced back to England. "It came like a tidal wave, first to the Atlantic States, where it gathered force and impetus and then flowed out over the hills and plains of the rest of the new world".[16]

From 1607 to 1776, the book was an important cultural implement in the English colonies in America. Political, social and cultural ideas and the scientific thought of Europe penetrated into the young American state with books. Thus colonial libraries, although few and far between, were present almost from the beginning. None of them reached a large size, but "their very existence is noteworthy and in these small collections we see the beginning of library history in the United States".[17]

Both during the latter part of the colonial period and afterward in the U.S., whenever there was an acknowledged need for libraries, they were established in form little different from those in England.[18] The real take off in the development of American libraries can be said to have occurred between 1850 and 1900, and Johnson and Harris have ably analysed the social, political and economic factors which made it possible.[19]

Librarianship in America made great strides in the twentieth century and library service in the U.S. today doubtless ranks with the best in the world.[20] A seminar report published by the International House of Japan in 1960, presents a picture of what American libraries look like to librarians from another part of the world where librarianship in its modern aspects was just beginning to emerge. The report states:

> Libraries in this country (U.S.A.) encourage greater freedom of thought and are more heavily used. . . . American libraries are invariably comfortable, useful, and attractive, they are conveniently located, well promoted, and their hours geared to public convenience.[21]

4. INDO-AMERICAN LIBRARY RELATIONS AS PART OF INTERNATIONAL LIBRARIANSHIP

The relations in the field of librarianship between India and the U.S. have to be viewed against this historical background. In a way, it is possible to examine these relations as part of what has come to be referred to as international librarianship.

International librarianship as an aspect of library science is relatively new and as such the term has been variously defined. "An extensive literature search reveals that the term *International Librarianship* has not been used frequently, and the most commonly used term is comparative librarianship".[22] Paraphrasing and somewhat modifying a definition of international education, Danton offers the following definition of international librarianship:

> International librarianship connotes the various kinds of relationships–intellectual, cultural and educational–among

> individuals and groups from two or more nations. . . . (It) refers to the various methods and practices of international cooperation, understanding, and exchange. Thus, the exchange of teachers and students, aid to underdeveloped countries, and teaching about foreign library systems all fall within the scope of this term.[23]

Parker defines the concept and role of international librarianship as consisting of "activities carried out among or between governmental or non-governmental institutions, organizations, groups or individuals of two or more nations, to promote, establish, develop, maintain and evaluate library, documentation and allied services, and librarianship and library profession generally, in any part of the world".[24] He also identifies three main functional areas under which the activities carried out under the heading of "international librarianship" may be subsumed. These are service provision, service promotion and information transfer.

5. UNITED STATES' INVOLVEMENT IN INTERNATIONAL LIBRARIANSHIP

Since its beginnings, the library movement in the U.S. has been interested in international interaction. It was as early as in September 1877 when thirteen U.S. librarians including Justin Winsor, American Library Association's (ALA) first president; William Frederick Poole, a founder of ALA; L. P. Smith, C. A. Cutter, Melvil Dewey and others, boarded the steamship, *Davonia*, as it prepared to leave New York on the return passage of its maiden voyage from Great Britain. It was the first official delegation of the newly formed ALA to an international meeting of librarians. The conference, which heralded a new era in librarianship, provided the opportunity for librarians from different countries to compare the growing library systems in Great Britain, France, Italy, Belgium and the U.S., and for Dewey and Cutter to present their cataloguing methods. Although it was not officially designated as an "international conference", the 1877 meeting was a landmark in the history of international library relations and only the first of many in which U.S. librarians played an influential role.[25] The second international conference was convened in London in 1897. A fifth of the more than 600 delegates who attended the conference represented libraries in the U.S.

In the decades between the turn of the century and the First World

War, U.S. librarians supported such projects as the *International Catalogue of Scientific Literature* (London, 1902-19), the *Conclium Bibliographicum* (Zurich, 1890), and the *Repertoire Bibliographique Universale* (Brussels, 1896); they also attended the 1910 Congress of Archivists and Librarians in Brussels. During the First World War years, there were ALA Committees on the importation of books, on promotion and cooperation in the development of printed catalogue cards in accordance with international agreements and also those dealing with other facets of the international relations. In the 1920s, 1930s and 1940s, important boards and committees came into being in the ALA covering, for example, activities like adult education, library extension, education for librarianship etc. and, under Carl H. Milam's leadership, international relations took on new meaning during these decades.

While U.S. librarians were thus involved in international librarianship in one way or another since 1877, very little was done prior to 1945 to directly assist libraries abroad. "It was only after the Second World War's close that a major thrust was made, by both government and non-government organizations, in rendering aid to overseas library development".[26]

The U.S. interest in international affairs since the Second World War can be attributed to several factors. Firstly, the war itself brought the American people forcibly into contact with the rest of the world to an extent which was quite new and in sharp contrast to the isolation of the 1930s. Secondly, the decline in power and influence of other world powers, such as Great Britain and France, created a leadership vacuum into which the U.S. quickly moved. Further, in the years after the Second World War, the U.S. accepted responsibility to assist the less fortunate countries of the world with social and economic development. This generated U.S. interest in foreign affairs. And finally, there was a growing recognition of and dissatisfaction with the parochialism of the American educational system. Especially after the war, educators and students in the U.S. became aware that curricula in all fields of knowledge were incomplete as they did not incorporate the experience of the whole of mankind. American research workers began to find in the rest of the world a laboratory for study with data not only of particular but of general interest.[27]

The January 1972 issue of *Library Trends*, devoted to "The influence of American librarianship abroad", gives a useful overview of post-World War II activities to that date and makes it clear that "not all U.S. participation in international library cooperation was funnelled through Unesco. There were other significant programs in their own right, such as USIA, the overseas programs of the Library of Congress, and the international activities of the American Library Association itself".[28]

6. UNITED STATES' INFLUENCE ON LIBRARIANSHIP IN OTHER COUNTRIES

As U.S. librarians were involved in "world librarianship" since 1877, American librarianship has influenced that in other countries which is evident from several published accounts such as those by Kildal, Liebaers, Brewster, Ludington, Shepard, Goodwin, Hewitt and Asheim.[29-36] About half a century ago, Kildal studied the American influence on European librarianship, whereas Liebaers brings out the impact of American and European librarianship upon each other. Brewster studies the U.S. library technical assistance abroad during the period from 1940 to 1970 and Ludington narrates the American contribution to foreign library establishment and rehabilitation. Shepard and Goodwin bring out the international dimensions of U.S. librarianship. Hewitt describes the U.S. services to library life abroad and Asheim points out the role of the U.S. in the librarianship in the developing countries.

Though all the above-mentioned studies are of general nature, a couple of studies involving particular countries have also been carried out. A quarter of a century ago, Danton studied the U.S. influence on Norwegian librarianship, stating in his preface that "the Norwegian adoption of American library philosophy and practice provides a towering example of international cultural influence".[37] In 1974, Suzuki, as his doctoral research, worked on *American Influence on the Development of Library Services in Japan during the Period 1860-1941*, showing that soon after the end of a long period of national seclusion (1853), Japanese educators and librarians chose American librarianship as their model. He points out that "American librarians have responded enthusiastically and generously toward the Japanese efforts, and, in turn, Japanese have always been well prepared and profited from their American library experience".[38]

Glazier describes the U.S. influence on Canadian universities and their libraries[39] and Burke looks at German librarianship from and American angle.[40] Danton makes a comparative study of German and

American university libraries so far as their book selection and collections are concerned.[41] Ryan studied the Soviet librarianship, bringing out the similarities between the modern Soviet library practice and the U.S. librarianship[42] and Reith gives a brief account of the library cooperation between the two countries–India and the U.S.[43]

7. NATURE OF THE PRESENT STUDY

The present study was prompted mainly by the editorial to the July 1982 issue of *International Library Review*, wherein Chandler states that "a comparative assessment of the impact of the extensive and wide range of cooperation programs (between the United States and India) would be of considerable value, particularly, if undertaken by an Indian individual or organization". Additionally, the present study can be considered as an attempt to unite one of the oldest traditions in librarianship in India with one of the best developed in the U.S.

It is in the light of these developments that one has to study library relations which emerged and were strengthened between the two countries during more than the past seventy-five years. This interaction between them started in as early as 1910 and was continued rather leisurely up to the end of the Second World War. After 1945, the U.S. became a prominent country in international affairs and, in due course of time, developed as one of the two Super Powers in the world. Naturally, she had much to offer to help develop Indian librarianship in a number of ways.

From the very beginning of this interaction, American library specialists came to India to work in various capacities such as librarians, library consultants, participants in seminars etc. A few of them also played a significant role in library science education in India. The U.S. also provided financial assistance to several institutions in India to develop their library collections. Reciprocally, library collections in some of the universities and research institutions in the U.S. could be developed because of the Library of Congress PL 480 Acquisitions Program. The Indian academic society at large was served to a great extent by the United States Information Service (USIS) libraries at various places in India. At the same time, theoretical work carried out in library field in India had some impact on the American library thinking. All these areas of interaction between the two countries are studied in the present work.

If one views the entire period of about eighty years from 1910, one may feel that during the initial stages, except Borden at Baroda and Dickinson at Lahore, not much existed by way of mutual relationship in the field between India and the U.S., and understandably so, for India still formed part of the British empire. After India's independence, and especially during the 1950s and 1960s, because of the India Wheat Loan Educational Exchange Programme, "the library profession (in India) made more progress. . . than during any other period".[44] After the 1960s once again the library relations between the two countries were deteriorating. It was in 1974 that the Governments of the U.S. and India, guided by a common desire to strengthen further the friendly relations between the two countries, agreed to constitute a Joint Commission on Economic, Commercial, Scientific, Technological, Educational and Cultural Cooperation. The Commission has played its role extremely well in strengthening the mutual relations. To strengthen still further the bilateral relations, the year 1984 was celebrated as the U.S. year in India and 1985 as India's in the U.S.

In substance, therefore, the present work is an attempt :

(1) to investigate (a) how and to what extent the work of American library specialists on assignment in India helped various institutions in India in their library matters, and (b) how the financial aid received from the U.S. has contributed to the enrichment of library collections in various institutions in the country;

(2) to measure the impact of visiting American library specialists on library science education in India;

(3) to find out how the Library of Congress PL 480 Acquisitions Program helped universities and other research institutions in the U.S. to strengthen their library collections with the additions of Indian material of research value and the kind of impact these acquisitions produced;

(4) to determine the role played by (a) the USIS libraries in India, (b) American Studies Research Center, and (c) American Institute of Indian Studies in meeting the library needs of the Indian clientele; and finally

(5) to assess objectively if there is any Indian influence on American library thinking.

NOTES AND REFERENCES

1. D. N. Marshall, *History of Libraries—Ancient and Medieval*, New Delhi, (1983): p. 105
2. *Ibid.*
3. J. N. Agrawal, "Libraries in ancient India," *Indian Librarian*, 8 (1953-54): 141-44.
4. S. N. Chakravorti, "Libraries in ancient times with special reference to India," *Indian Librarian*, 9 (1954-55): 49-57.
5. Raghunandan Shastri, "Book-activity in ancient India," *Indian Librarian*, 6 (1951-52): 16-18.
6. N. C. Chakravarty, "Librarianship in India," *I. L. A. Bulletin*, 4 (1968): 37-46.
7. Anis Khurshid, "Growth of libraries in India," *International Library Review*, 4 (1972): 21-65.
8. N. B. Inamdar and M. R. Riswadkar, "India," in *International Handbook of Contemporary Developments in Librarianship*, Westport, Connecticut, 1981, pp. 183-99.
9. Chakravorti, *op. cit.*
10. J. H. Shera, "The literature of American library history," *Library Quarterly*, 15 (1945): 1-24.
11. Sister M. Anne John O'Loughlin, *The Emergence of American Librarianship—A Study of Influences Evident in 1876*, Ph. D. thesis, Columbia University, 1971.
12. J. C. Colson, "The writing of American library history, 1876-1976," *Library Trends*, 25 (1976-77): 7-21.
13. Douglas W. Bryant, "Mid-Century American librarianship—Examination and experimentation," *Libri*, 7 (1958): 233-52.
14. Robert Vosper, "A century abroad," *College and Research Libraries*, 37 (1976): 514-30.
15. Herman Liebaers, "Books, libraries and librarians—European and American style," *Journal of Library History*, 8 (1973): 18-22.
16. Wilhelm Munthe, *American Librarianship from a European Angle—An Attempt at an Evaluation of Policies and Activities*, Chicago, 1939, p. 1.
17. K. H. Bendigeri, "Library movement in U.S.A. " *Timeless Fellowship*, 9 (1974-75): 1-11.
18. W. Boyd Rayward, "Librarianship in the new world and the old—Some points of contact," *Library Trends*, 25 (1976-77): 209-26.
19. Elmer D. Johnson and Michael H. Harris, *History of Libraries in the Western World*, Metuchen (N. J.), 1976, p. 265.
20. "Editorial," *Library Journal*, 85 (1960): 4114.
21. Haruki Amatsuchi *et al.*, *American Libraries—Report of the U.S. Field Seminar on Library Reference Services for Japanese Librarians*, Tokyo, 1960, pp. 14-15.
22. Naimuddin Qureshi, Comparative and international librarianship—An analytical approach," *Unesco Journal of Information Science, Librarianship and Archives Administration*, 2 (1980): 22-28.
23. J. Periam Danton, "Definitions of comparative and international library

science," in *Comparative and International Library Science* edited by John F. Harvey, Metuchen (N. J.), 1977, pp. 3-14.

24. J. Stephen Parker, "International librarianship—A reconnaisance," *Journal of Librarianship*, 6 (1974): 219-32.
25. Vivian D. Hewitt, "Services to library life abroad," in *A Century of Service—Librarianship in the United States and Canada*, Chicago, 1976, pp. 321-40.
26. Miles M. Jackson, "Library development abroad," *Library Journal*, 91 (1966) ; 1354-61.
27. C. D. Goodwin, "International dimension—international involvement of American libraries," in *Libraries at Large—Tradition, Innovation and the National Interest*, New York, 1969, pp. 559-89.
28. Cecil K. Byrd, "Introduction," *Library Trends*, 20 (1971-72): 475-77.
29. Arne Kildal, "American influence on European librarianship," *Library Quarterly*, 7 (1937): 196-210.
30. Herman Liebaers, "The impact of American and European librarianship upon each other," in *Libraries and the life of the Mind in America—Addresses Delivered at the Centennial Celebration of the American Library Association*, Chicago, 1977, pp. 65-83.
31. Beverly J. Brewster, *American Overseas Library Technical Assistance, 1940-1970*, Metuchen (N. J.), 1976, pp. 434.
32. Flora B. Ludington, "The American contribution to foreign library establishment and rehabilitation," *Library Quarterly*, 24 (1954): 192-204.
33. M. D. Shepard, "International dimensions of U.S. librarianship," *A. L. A. Bulletin*, 62 (1968): 699-710.
34. Goodwin, *op. cit.*
35. Hewitt, *op. cit.*
36. Lester Asheim, *Librarianship in the Developing Countries*, Urbana, 1966, pp. 95.
37. J. Periam Danton, *United States Influence on Norwegian Librarianship, 1890-1940*, Berkeley, 1957, pp. 91.
38. Yukihisa Suzuki, *American Influence on the Development of Library Services in Japan, 1860-1941*, Ph. D. thesis, University of Michigan, 1974.
39. Kenneth M. Glazier, "United States' influence on Canadian universities and their libraries," *College and Research Libraries*, 28 (1967): 311-16.
40. Redmond Burke, "German librarianship from an American angle," *Library Quarterly*, 22 (1952): 180-93.
41. J. Periam Danton, Book selection and collections—A Comparison of German and American University Libraries, New York, 1961, pp. 188.
42. Frederick Ryan, "Librarianship Soviet style," *Library Journal*, 106 (1981): 2360-64.
43. David Reith, "Indo-American cooperation in librarianship," *International Library Review*, 14 (1982): 263-81.
44. J. S. Sharma, *The Substance of Library Science*, Bombay, 1965, p. 44.

2

AMERICAN LIBRARY SPECIALISTS ASSIGNED TO INDIA

1. INTRODUCTION

In the bilateral relationship between India and the U.S. in the field of librarianship, it is undeniable that the U.S. has contributed far more than India has been able to reciprocate. India has received great help from the U.S. in numerous ways. A large number of American library specialists came to India to work in various institutions and render advice on library matters; many educational and research institutions received substantial grants under the India Wheat Loan Educational Exchange Program and also from other philanthropic organizations; many Indian librarians were given an opportunity to be trained in the U.S.; a lot of Indian books were procured by libraries in the U.S. under the Library of Congress PL 480 Acquisitions Program. In the chapters that follow, an attempt is made to study these various aspects in detail. The present chapter deals with the American Library specialists (consultants) who had been to India during the Last eight decades.

According to the dictionary, the term 'consultant' means a person who is consulted for his expert advice in one or another aspect of work. However, it is not used here in such a restricted sense. The *Foreign Service Directory of American Librarians* includes advisers or consultants, conference delegates, students, lecturers, acquisition programme participants, librarians who were abroad with some research project or with some short-term assignment by their own institutions, Peace Corps volunteers and others.[1] The present account, therefore, includes all these categories of American library personnel who visited India for one reason or another under the generic term 'consultants'.

The steady development of a body of consultants and the practice of consulting has occurred within the library and information science since the 1930s. "Particularly since the Second World War, there have been a number of outstanding librarians who have made a second career of. . . library consultation."[2] So far as American librarians abroad were concerned, there are earlier isolated examples of their employment as consultants or advisers; however, "their use on anything like a regular basis was first undertaken in the years between the two World Wars by the Carnegie Corporation of New York, which sent a number of leading British and American librarians on advisory missions to East, West and Southern Africa, West Indies, Australia and New Zealand in connection with its programme of aid to overseas library development."[3] This is evident from the fact that whereas slightly more than fifty librarians participated in overseas work between 1876-1940, their number rose to 1,966 between 1946-55 and soared to 2,793 between 1956-65.[4]

It is rather difficult to locate exact figures on the total number of American librarians involved in overseas work at any given time; however, certain attempts in this direction are worth mentioning. Foremost among these attempts, in chronological order, is the contribution of A. C. Hansen, a member of A. L. A. Council, who, in 1944, developed a roster of some 585 American librarians qualified in one respect or another for foreign service.[5] Another noteworthy attempt is the *Foreign Service Directory of American Librarians* mentioned earlier. It gives information about American librarians who had been abroad to provide expertise. The third edition of the *Directory*, which was published in 1967, includes information up to 1965 only and arranges in its 109 pages, 1,009 entries about American librarians abroad.

2. AMERICAN LIBRARY SPECIALISTS ASSIGNED TO INDIA

In the Indian context, the earliest example of employing an American librarian as consultant was in the first decade of the present century when "H. H. the Maharaja Gaekwad, on his second tour in America in 1910, engaged the services of a well-known and far-sighted library expert, the late Mr. W. A. Borden, and made him the first Director of the Library Department of the Baroda State".[6] Since then a large number of American library specialists have come to India in one capacity or another. Table 2.1 shows the number of American library specialists who came to India under various categories.

TABLE 2.1: American Library Specialists Assigned to India
(Categorywise)

	Category		Number of specialists
1.	Specialists as librarians/library directors		37
2.	Specialists under different programmes		20
	India Wheat Loan Educational Exchange Program	7	
	Library of Congress PL 480 Acquisition Program	13	
3.	Specialists at individual institutions		23
	University of Delhi, Delhi	3	
	University of Rajasthan, Jaipur	1	
	Documentation Research and Training Centre, Bangalore	6	
	Indian Institute of Technology, Kanpur	6	
	American Studies Research Centre, Hyderabad	6	
	College of Engineering, Guindy	1	
4.	Specialists at agricultural institutions		7
5.	Specialists with short-term assignments		3
6.	Specialists as delegates to seminars/conferences		28
	Unesco Seminar, Delhi, 1960	1	
	Third International Study Conference on Classification Research, Bombay, 1975	11	
	Indo-US. Seminars on Scientific and Technical Information:		
	Second seminar, Bangalore, 1977	9	
	Third Seminar, Delhi, 1980	7	
	International Conference on Ranganathan's Philosophy, Delhi, 1985	—	
7.	Others		27
		Total:	145

Note: Names of these specialists are provided in Appendices I-VII.

TABLE 2.2: American Library Specialists Assigned to India
(Periodwise)

Period	Number of specialists
Before 1950	11
During 1950-1959	23
During 1960-1969	51
During 1970-1979	28
During 1980-1988	27
Information not available	5
Total:	145[7]

It can be seen from Table 2.2 that very few American specialists came to India before her independence and understandably so.

3. SPECIALISTS AS LIBRARY DIRECTORS/LIBRARIANS

Thirty-seven American library specialists came to India to work as library directors/librarians. Of these, the first two, viz. W. A. Borden and A. D. Dickinson, worked in India during the first quarter of the present century and the remaining thirty-five during the span of about four decades from 1944 to 1988. Out of these thirty-five, twenty-four worked as library directors, librarians or deputy librarians in the libraries attached to American Centers (United States Information Service) at Bombay, Calcutta, Delhi, Lucknow and Madras.

3.1 **W. A. Borden**

"The first stimulating influence on Indian libraries came from abroad as early as 1910 when the Maharaja of Baroda appointed William Alanson Borden. . . as Director of the State Department of Libraries, Baroda".[8] The Maharaja, referred to as the "Carnegie of India",[9] engaged Borden and sent him to Baroda with the commission of opening free public libraries in the Baroda State.

Before coming to India, Borden had wide experience in librarianship in the U.S. He studied library technique for three years under Charles A. Cutter, one of the founders of modern librarianship. Borden had also worked as a lecturer in the Columbia University Library School under Melvil Dewey for three years. As librarian of the Young Men's Institute, New Haven, he had introduced certain special features there, such as a children's room, a library school and a system of travelling libraries. All his manifold activities were an appropriate preparation for his great work–the introduction of the free popular library system in Baroda.

Borden laid the foundation of a state-wide public library system in the state of Baroda, perhaps unheard of in those days in the eastern part of the world. About this library system, he himself has stated:

> . . . I determined to introduce into Baroda what we in the United States have recognized as a goal to be ultimately attained, but which we have not yet reached. I mean a system of centrally located book storehouses, each surrounded by a network of small, inter-depending libraries. These small libraries to have the books

commonly called for and the storehouses to supplement these small collections. This has been done and the result is now known in India as the Baroda System.[10]

Borden adds that, "If there is any value in this library cooperation throughout a large state let it be remembered that it was first introduced, not in the home of the modern library movement, our own country, but way down in India, 10,000 miles from here".[11]

Among other contributions which Borden made during his three-year stay at Baroda, a mention should be made of systematic classification and cataloguing, open access, children's library, book mobiles and library training classes for the staff working under him. Further, as he himself mentions, ". . . In addition, I have induced the members of my staff to start the Baroda Library Club, which meets monthly and which already has a reputable membership. They have also started a quarterly magazine, devoted to library matter, called *The Library Miscellany*. Furthermore, in the way of library extension, we have established a Visual Instruction Branch, for the benefit of the many who cannot read. This branch has four cinematographs and is showing educative films in the villages and towns of the State–free of course".[12] He did all this long before anyone thought of technical cooperative missions.

Borden must be given credit for the establishment of the first public library network in India, which was his greatest contribution to Indian librarianship. It was thirty-five years after his pioneering work at Baroda that the second network of libraries appeared in India in 1948 with the Madras Public Libraries Act becoming operative. Borden anticipated and realized mobile libraries, children's libraries, etc.–things which were completely unknown to people in India at that time. He was too far ahead of his period in introducing audio-visual aids in public libraries, especially for the benefit of illiterate people in India. He also deserves credit for starting *The Library Miscellany*, the first professional journal, and also the first forum in the form of Baroda Library Club. It was truly the beginning of library profession in India since his work at Baroda had an abiding influence on several libraries in the country. Indeed, with the encouragement of the Maharaja of Baroda, he was a pioneer in the neglected field of librarianship.

3.2 A. D. Dickinson

Another, even more stimulating, influence came to India from the U.S.

in 1915 when Asa Don Dickinson was appointed as Librarian of the Punjab University at Lahore (now in Pakistan).[13]

The history of the Punjab University Library dates back to 1873 when the University College acquired from Sir Donald Mcleod a collection of 2,000 volumes. This was the nucleus round which the University library came into being as a result of the Universities Act of 1904.[14] Having acquired a new site in 1912, the library progressed rapidly. "The next logical step was the reorganization of the library (for which) the services of Mr. Asa Don Dickinson . . . were acquired . . . He took infinite pains to ensure that the various processes of reorganization should proceed unbroken from beginning to end, that no gap should be left unfilled which would prevent the library from functioning on new lines at the opportune time".[15] Though Dickinson stayed at Lahore only for a year (1915-16), during that short period "the library was overhauled, reclassified and recatalogued".[16] "The organization on the American system (which was) considered to be a remote possibility by the University Commission in 1904 was complete as if by magic by the end of 1916".[17]

Dickinson's other contributions include starting a library training class, introducing open access system in the University library, publishing his *Panjab Library Primer* and founding the Punjab Library Association. The change from the closed shelf system to the open access system was so phenomenal that it inspired Labhu Ram to say that "the barriers between readers and books were removed for the first time in the Punjab".[18]

With the assistance of Lala Mukand Lal Bhatia, Dickinson brought out *Panjab Library Primer*,[19] perhaps the first library manual of its kind in India, for the guidance of librarians all over the Punjab in the reorganization of their libraries. As he states in the preface, "This little book is the fruit of a decade's experience among American libraries, modified by a year's acquaintance with conditions peculiar to India".[20] The *Primer* is just what its name implies, a primer of library organization and management and is "an excellent handbook for inexperienced librarians in the public, college and school libraries in India".[21] As Dickinson himself believed, "the average Punjab librarian (who is generally a college matriculate but only rarely a college graduate) by a diligent study of these pages will find himself able to improve very materially the conditions in his library".[22]

Dickinson also introduced the Dewey Decimal Classification (DDC) in the University library which helped in organizing the collection in a simple yet systematic manner. The DDC became so popular in India, that she became the largest user of it in the continent (please see Para 7.1 on page 33 under Sarah K. Vann).

Further, in order to initiate a library movement in the Punjab, Dickinson founded the Punjab Library Association. The Association did a considerable work for some time, but could not exist for long after his departure.[23]

Dickinson's one-year tenure at the Punjab University Library was significant for two things. He introduced university librarianship as it is understood today, and instituted university-based library education in India.

The impact of these two first American librarians cannot be described better than in the words of Ludington who says that "the results of the work of William A. Borden in Baroda and Asa Don Dickinson in Lahore were still apparent after thirty years when I visited libraries in India".[24]

3.3 Katharine S. Diehl

Katharine S. Diehl worked at Serampore College as librarian during 1961-62. As she has recorded, "On September 1, 1961, I joined the staff of Serampore College (Serampore, West Bengal, India) as bibliographer. This project was made possible by a grant from the Lilly Endowment, Inc., and involved the identification of every item in the 'old library', the Carey Library of Serampore College, as well as the very minute cataloging of the books and pamphlets and newspapers published in Greater India before December 31, 1850".[25]

> Her second visit [to India] was in 1967 as Senior Fellow, American Institute of Indian Studies, Calcutta, from September 1967 to September 1969. On the expiry of this fellowship, and since the Government of India required that all foreigners doing research in any subject should get affiliated with an Indian academic institution, she got herself affiliated to the University Library, University of Bombay.[26]
>
> Her main interest of study was early printing and imprints and among her publications are included *Religions, Mythologies, Folklores–An Annotated Bibliography* (New York, 1956), *Early Indian Imprints–An Exhibition from the William Carey Historical Library of Serampore* (Serampore, 1962), *Early Indian Imprints* (New York, 1964) and *Primary Sources for 16th-19th Century*

Studies in Bengal, Orissa and Bihar Libraries–Seminar Papers (Calcutta, 1971). Her projected nine-volume publication on *Printing in the East Indies up to 1850*, dealing with Batavia, Ceylon, the extreme South of India, Bombay, Calcutta, Orissa, the North East of China, Australia, Madras, and a bibliography of every pre-1850 Asian Imprint is awaited.

3.4 Specialists as Library Directors/Librarians at American Centers

A large number of American library specialists–thirty-four in all–came to India under the USIS, to work as library directors/librarians in American Centers at different places in the country. The contribution of the USIS libraries is discussed in Chapter 6. The first USIS library in India was established at Calcutta in 1943 and those at Bombay, Delhi and Madras in 1944, 1946 and 1947 respectively. Libraries were established at other places also, viz. Banglore, Hyderabad, Lucknow, Patna and Trivandrum. These were, however, closed down in 1970.

Table 2.3 shows the number of library directors/librarians who worked at American Centers in India between 1944 and 1988. Though it is difficult to evaluate the contribution of these specialists individually, the high reputation these libraries enjoy in India is certainly the fruit of their untiring efforts as well as their considerable abilities.

TABLE 2.3: Number of Library Directors/Librarians in USIS Libraries in India during 1944-1988

Centre	Number of Library Directors/ Librarians *
Bombay	4
Calcutta	7
Delhi	12 **
Lucknow	1
Madras	7
Place not mentioned	3
	34

* Their names are given in Appendix I.

** Of these 12, one worked as Press Secretary, two as cultural attache and three as Libraries and Book Services Officers.

It should be stated in passing that Indian librarians of those days became rather disconcertingly aware that 59 per cent of the visiting library directors/librarians–twenty in number–were women. Library Centers at Bombay, Calcutta (except one director) and Madras were always headed by women. The point is noteworthy because at a time when India was not much developed in the field of librarianship and not many Indian women had yet even heard of the library profession, women in the U.S. were already professionally educated and were regarded as competent enough to manage a library and lead a library programme. The feminization of librarianship in the U.S. has been a prominent feature of the profession since as early as 1887.[27]

Among experts who were connected with the USIS in India but did not act as librarians were Juliane M. Heyman who worked as Press Secretary in the USIS during 1951-52; Thomas S. Cleveland who was the Cultural Attache from 1960 to 1963; Wayne M. Hartwell who, in addition to being a librarian, also worked as the Cultural Attache from 1946 to 1951, though the place where he actually worked is not mentioned in the Directory; Michael B. Pipkin who worked as the Libraries and Book Services Officer in the American Center, New Delhi, followed by Donald C. Hausrath, who occupied that position up to August 1987. Since then, Ann Donovan Lee is acting in that capacity.

4. SPECIALISTS UNDER DIFFERENT PROGRAMMES

India Wheat Loan Educational Exchange Program and the Library of Congress PL 480 Acquisitions Program were the two U.S. Government-sponsored programmes in which a total of twenty American library specialists worked in India. The first programme under which seven specialists came to India was in operation during 1954-62; whereas the second has been in operation since 1962 and thirteen specialists were involved in its activities in India. These programmes are discussed in detail in Chapters 3 and 5 respectively.

4.1 Specialists under India Wheat Loan Educational Exchange Program

As stated earlier, during the eight-year period (1954-62) of the Wheat Loan Program, seven American library specialists came to India in its operation. The Wheat Loan Office in Delhi was "staffed by two library specialists, Lucile Dudgeon during the first year and Beatrice Holt from 1955 to 1961, who administered the grants to university and research libraries to purchase books, periodicals, and selected non-print materials".[28] The other five specialists were John Alden, Archie McNeal, Jennings Wood, Laurence J. Kipp, and Cecilia R. Kipp.

4.1.1 John Alden: John Alden of the Boston Public Library and a well-known specialists in book preservation and book binding, stayed in India for three months, during which period the National Library of India arranged his visits to various academic and manuscript libraries in different parts of the country–Delhi, Patna, Calcutta, Madras, Tanjore, Trivandrum, Mysore, Hyderabad, Bombay and Pune– "to observe and report on them so that the authorities running them might know the true state of affairs and take steps to put their house in order".[29] After his visits to libraries at these places, he submitted his report to the National Library on 8 May 1958.[30] He also gave a course of lectures on book preservation and book binding problems to a group of librarians drawn from all over the country. The most important achievement of Alden's visit "was the creation of an atmosphere in the library world that book preservation was a major and essential responsibility of libraries and librarians".[31]

4.1.2 Archie McNeal and Jennings Wood: Archie McNeal of the University of Miami, Florida, was in India during 1957-58. He was the only librarian to serve with an American team on general education and has published his observations on some of the academic and research libraries in India.[32] Jennings Wood's visit, to India from December 1958 through April 1959 was concerned more with the Library of Congress PL 480 Acquisitions Program.

4.1.3 Laurence J. and Cecilia R. Kipps: Laurence J. Kipp and Cecilia Rae Kipp of the Harvard Business School were in India for eight months. In August 1961, at the end of their visit, they submitted a report[33] to the Indian and American librarians, which is an "excellent assessment of the Indian university libraries and librarians during the. . . decade".[34]

During their stay in India, the Kipps undertook to (i) evaluate the Wheat Loan Program as it involved books, libraries and librarians; (ii) serve as consultants to libraries they visited; (iii) plan and direct four workshops for librarians; and (iv) report upon their own programme.[35] They intended "to ascertain the basic problems faced by such libraries and try to solve them through the efforts of the librarians themselves",[36] for which purpose they visited a number of university, research and academic libraries tendering advice, wherever sought, on library problems. They also officiated as Directors of the four zonal workshops, organized under the auspices of the Ministry of Education (Government of India), the University Grants Commission and the Wheat Loan Office.

4.2 Specialists under the Library of Congress PL 480 Acquisitions Program.

Thirteen American library specialists worked in India under the PL 480 program during the past three decades in the capacity of either the Director or Assistant Director in the New Delhi office. Though it is difficult to evaluate their work individually, their work in general in procuring Indian material for libraries in the U.S. successfully, speaks about their contribution. The success and the impact of this programme on the U.S. as well as on India is discussed at length in Chapter 4.

5. SPECIALISTS AT INDIVIDUAL INSTITUTIONS

Twenty-two American library specialists came to India to work or to provide expertise or to deliver lectures at six individual institutions, viz. (i) University of Delhi, Delhi; (ii) University of Rajasthan, Jaipur; (iii) Documentation Research and Training Centre, Bangalore; (iv) Indian Institute of Technology, Kanpur; (v) American Studies Research Centre, Hyderabad; and (vi) College of Engineering, Guindy. Out of these twenty-two, three worked at the University of Delhi, one each at the University of Rajasthan and the College of Engineering, Guindy, five delivered lectures at the DRTC, Bangalore and six each were assigned to the IIT, Kanpur, and the American Studies Research Centre, Hyderabad.

5.1 University of Delhi, Delhi

During the 1960s three American library specialists have been associated with the University of Delhi. Carl M. White worked at the university in 1965, followed by Morris Gelfand in the subsequent year and George S. Bonn three years later.

5.1.1 Carl M. White: Carl M. White, Programme Specialist in Library Administration in the University of California, visited the

University of Delhi to serve as a short-term consultant under the Ford Foundation Grant. The sole purpose of his visit was to study the working of the University Library and report on its possible development into an ideal university library. His report[37] deserves more than a cursory treatment.

As White himself mentions in his letter of Transmittal to the Vice-Chancellor of the University, "The report in hand has been prepared . . . to dig out relevant information about the University's library problems and report it in a form suitable for fruitful consideration by the authorities who are responsible for the future of the University".[38] In preparing his report, White met several persons including C. D. Deshmukh, Vice-Chancellor; B. N. Ganguli, Pro-Vice-Chancellor; heads of the various departments in the University; and many librarians including S. R. Ranganathan, B. S. Kesavan, N. M. Ketkar, Kamla Kapoor, S. P. Phadnis, D. R. Kalia, Girja Kumar, Dhanapat Rai, N. K. Goil, John C. Crawford (Director of the American Library Book Procurement Center).[39]

The *Report* which has a unique place in the history of university librarianship in India did attract the attention of librarians in India and abroad, which is evident from the reviews or editorials which appeared hot on its heels.[40-45] It is divided into nine chapters and it records a total of ninety-four recommendations which supplement one another. True that these recommendations were "numerous enough to require a good deal of sustained attention to get them in mind and hold them in mind long enough for the university to take action on them".[46] Unfortunately, the University and the Government ran into difficulties in getting a firm agreement from the Government side to carry out the recommendations.[47] However, "the permanent value to India of the survey report . . . will hinge on the understanding which Indian librarians gain of the method of approach used".[48]

Even Malcolm M. Willey and J. Arthur Branch (both from Ford Foundation, who visited India in 1968, appreciated the White Report by pointing out to the University authorities in India that "to understand a library survey in depth, the study of the University of Delhi Library by Dr. Carl White, published in 1966, can be recommended as a model".[49] They further recommend to the University authorities that "it would be useful, as background material and as an indication of the scope and importance of an analysis of the library, to have the general philosophy and recommendation of the White Report summarized".[50]

White made a significant contribution in the form of his Report to library profession in India in general and to university librarianship and the University of Delhi Library in particular. His report "prescribed tremendous responsibilities on the Delhi University Librarian and made an evolutionary and generic impact on the library scene in Delhi University".[51] Before accepting the assignment, White had wide experience as director of three major libraries in the U.S.–the University of North Carolina, the University of Illinois and Columbia University. He knew well that the situation in India would be quite different from that in the U.S. The fact that he had a wide range of consultations with several individuals in the university community and that his report was backed by an impressive amount of supporting data in the form of statistics and opinions from faculty and librarians on the various aspects of library situation shows his deep interest in university librarianship in India.

White recommended academic status for the university librarian, making him answerable directly to the Vice-Chancellor for the performance of his duties and turned the library committee into an advisory body. The fact that that status is accorded to university librarians in India today is due in no small measure to White. The *Report* is the only model available to librarians in India for undertaking an evaluative study of their services. Indeed, the value of White's contribution to university librarianship in India cannot be overstated.

5.1.2 Morris A. Gelfand and George S. Bonn: Morris A. Gelfand and George S. Bonn worked in the University of Delhi during the years 1966 and 1968 respectively, as visiting professors of library science under the Rockefeller Project of Advanced Training in Library Administration. Their contribution is more or less related to library science education in India and hence it is discussed in Chapter 4.

5.2 University of Rajasthan, Jaipur

Only one American library specialist viz. Carl W. Hintz worked at the University of Rajasthan as a Visiting Professor on Fulbright grant. Like Gelfand and Bonn, Hintz's contribution is also related to library science education in India and is described in Chapter 4.

5.3 Documentation Research and Training Centre (DRTC) Bangalore

Six professors visited the Documentation Research and Training

Centre at Bangalore : Jesse H. Shera in 1967,[52] Pauline A. Atherton in 1970, Jean M. Perreault in 1975, Patrick R. Penland in 1976, Charles P. Bourne in 1978 and Eugene Garfield in 1983. Except Penland, the others had been to DRTC to deliver the Sarada Ranganathan Lectures organized by the Sarada Ranganathan Endowment for Library Science, founded in 1961 by S. R. Ranganathan and Sarada Ranganathan. Table 2.4 provides the details of the Sarada Ranganathan lectures delivered by them.

TABLE 2.4: Sarada Ranganathan Lectures by American Professors

	Speaker	Year	Topic
1.	Jesse H. Shera	1967	Sociological foundations of librarianship.
2.	Pauline A. Atherton	1970	Putting knowledge to work: An American view of the five laws of library science.
3.	Jean M. Perreault	1975	The idea of order in bibliography.
4.	Charles P. Bourne	1978	Technology in support of library science and information service.
5.	Eugene Garfield	1983	Citation indexes, co-citation analysis and clustering and third world research

The choice of these speakers is itself a testimony to their eminence in the American library world, and, as can be seen from the topics on which they spoke, the state of the art in a variety of areas in librarianship was brought home to Indian librarians by their lectures. It is a happy practice of the Endowment to publish the Sarada Ranganathan lectures, and all but the last of the above lectures are thus fortunately available to a far wider readership.[53-56]

5.3.1 Pauline A. Atherton: In addition to delivering the Sarada Ranganathan Lectures, the visiting professors also have some other contribution to their credit. For example, Atherton was the main speaker at the inauguration of the IATLIS (Indian Association of Teachers of Library and Information Science) Seminar on teaching methods of library science, delivered lectures to the DRTC students and faculty, and addressed the students and faculty of library science of Women's Polytechnic, Bangalore and the Department of Library Science, University of Madras.[57]

5.3.2 Jean M. Perreault: Perreault gave lectures to DRTC trainees on the "Structure and compatibility of UDC and LC class numbers, attended the NISSAT[58] symposium at Delhi and spoke to library school students at Delhi, Hyderabad and Madras.[59]

5.3.3 Charles P. Bourne: Bourne participated as a Resource Person in the All-India Seminar on primary communication in science and technology in India, Bangalore and paid visits to Delhi and Madras. At Delhi, he had discussions with the officials of the Department of Science and Technology, Government of India, delivered a lecture to the staff and students of INSDOC and gave a public lecture on computer-assisted reference service. At Madras, he visited the libraries of Madras University, Indian Institute of Technology and Central Leather Research Institute, and gave a public lecture on technology of information.[60]

Bourne's other noteworthy activities included discussions with various organizations about the possibility of their using the DIALOG search service, and a series of online searches that he did for several of the DRTC students and faculty, in order to provide computer print-outs with background information in their own thesis projects.[61]

5.3.4 Eugene Garfield: Garfield visited India thrice–sometime before 1969, then in 1974 and finally in 1983. His third visit was to deliver the Sarada Ranganathan lectures on citation indexes, co-citation analysis and clustering, and third world research. Lecturing at Madras University later, he covered the same subjects again, but presented an additional talk that related his work to Ranganathan. His tribute to Ranganathan was published in *New Trends in International Librarianship*.[62]

5.3.5. Patrick R. Penland: Patrick R. Penland, an expert in communication science from the University of Pittsburgh, visited India twice, during February-March 1976 and again during January-April 1985. In 1976, he delivered a course of five lectures at DRTC on various aspects of communication.[63] He also delivered a couple of lectures at the Bangalore University and the Indian Institute of Science. He paid visits to library schools at Mysore University, Mysore and Kerala University, Trivandrum and also INSDOC, Delhi, to deliver lectures on the topics concerning communication.[64]

Penland's links with Indian libraries and librarianship were not over after his return from India in March 1976, as he continued to work for Indian librarianship in one way or another. He is a contributor, editor and consultant to the *ALIS bulletin*, published by the Academy of Library and Information Science, Trivandrum and also a contributor and editorial consultant to the *Library Progress International*, published by the Multanimal Modi College, U. P. He is a Ph.D. adjudicator at the Andhra University, Waltair and the University of Poona.[65]

Penland's second visit to India during January-April 1985 was to work as a Fulbright Visiting Professor at the SHPT School of Library Science, SNDT women's University, Bombay. In addition to working as the Fulbright Professor, he attended the international seminar on "The changing technological environment and development of workforce: Directions for library and information science education", organized by the Osmania University, Hyderabad. He also paid visits to SNDT Women's University branch at Pune, University of Poona, Pune, National Library, Calcutta and Panjab University, Chandigarh, to deliver lectures on various topics related to library science and communication.

5.4 Indian Institute of Technology, Kanpur

Indian Institute of Technology (IIT) at Kanpur is a peculiar Indo-American joint programme, the goal of which was to develop a high-level research institute at Kanpur. A team of three professors from the Massachusetts Institute of Technology (MIT) visited IIT, Kanpur; in February 1961. As a result of the initiative of the MIT, a consortium of five universities and four Institutes of Technology in the U.S. was formed. In January 1962, a contract was signed between the U.S. Government and the Educational Services Incorporated for coordinating and channellising the assistance to the IIT, Kanpur.[67]

The Steering Committee of the Kanpur Indo-American Program, at its meeting held in Purdue on 22nd September, 1962, finalized the library collaboration proposals and Purdue University was entrusted with the task of systematically assembling and shipping the library material to India, and helping in library organization.[68] Accordingly, during 1962-68, Purdue University, one of the participants in the consortium, under AID (Agency for International Development) contract, undertook IIT library development. "This project involved purchasing, cataloguing and processing duplicate copies of all books ordered for Purdue's own engineering, mathematics, chemistry, and physics libraries, as well as recataloguing, at Purdue, the Kanpur campus library's old collections from typed copies of the catalogue cards shipped from India to Purdue".[69] During the span of eight years, 1962-70, six American library specialists, as shown in Table 2.5, had been to the IIT, Kanpur, either for short-term assignments or for longer periods.

TABLE 2.5: American Library Specialists at IIT, Kanpur

	Name of the specialist	Period of assignment
1.	Oliver C. Dunn	1962; 1964; 1966; 1968
2.	George Meluch	1962-64
3.	Richard Funkhouser	1964-66
4.	Robert Cain	1966-67
5.	Margaret Berg	1966-67
6.	Irma Johnson	1968-70

The annual reports of IIT, Kanpur, covering the period from 1961 to 1971, put more emphasis on the number of books added to the library, but mention the work of these American specialists only very briefly. However, certain points deserve due mention.

Oliver C. Dunn, the then Associate Director of Purdue University Library, made a number of short-term consulting trips to IIT, as shown above, to assist the library development work and to have "extensive discussions with the library staff on various library matters, e.g. acquisition, technical processing, circulation and reference services".[70]

Both Dunn and Meluch prepared their reports on the library at IIT, Kanpur. Dunn's report appeared in *ESI quarterly report* (Winter-Spring 1964), whereas that of Meluch was perhaps only mimeographed. Further, some of these specialists also worked as members of the Library Committee of the IIT, Kanpur, which was constituted for the first time in 1965-66. As the annual reports of the IIT for these years reveal, Funkhouser was a member of the Library Committee in 1965-66, Cain in 1966-67, and Berg and Johnson in 1967-68 and 1968-70 respectively. Johnson also gave her *Observations at mid-term* on the Library, her comments *on the appointment of IIT Librarian* and her *Suggestion* to improve the activities of the library. These official documents must have definitely helped the IIT, Kanpur to improve the status as well as the services of its library. The contribution of these library specialists undoubtedly enabled the IIT, which itself is modelled after the MIT, to have one of the best libraries in the country. Indian librarians now at the IIT deserve full credit for keeping up its reputation.

5.5 American Studies Research Centre, Hyderabad

From its establishment in 1964 till today, the American Studies Research Centre (ASRC) at Hyderabad has benefited from the expertise of six American library specialists, viz. Dorothy L. Clark, John R. and Margaret R. Russels, Jo Manning and Ronald and Ellen Chapmans. Clark was associated with the ASRC for the comparatively longer period of thirteen years from 1966 to 1979 whereas Russells and Chapmans spent about seven to eight months at the ASRC and Manning visited it for a few days only.

5.5.1 Dorothy L. Clark: After working in the American Centre at Bombay for a decade, i.e. during 1957-66, Clark joined the American Studies Research Centre as assistant librarian in 1966, when the Centre's library was beginning to be set up. From 1966 to 1974, she worked as assistant librarian and from 1975 to 1979 as Acting Librarian. Over the years, she made a signal contribution in making ASRC a valuable resource for many. After thirteen years of distinguished and dedicated service, she retired from the Centre in June 1979. Nearly every aspect of the library activity–from acquisition to classification and cataloguing to the thoughtful and imaginative book displays on the bulletin board–today bears the stamp of her work. Hundreds of scholars from all over the country, have recorded their gratitude to her for her valuable assistance in their studies and research. It is a measure of the recognition of her contribution that the Centre felt it fitting to express in its *Newsletter* its deep appreciation and gratitude for all that she did for its library.[71]

5.5.2. John R. and Margaret R. Russell: John R. Russell, Director of Libraries, University of Rochester, visited ASRC as library consultant from September 1966 to March 1967. Before coming to the ASRC, Russell had wide experience and responsibility in collection development and planning library buildings at the University of Rochester for many years. His visit to the ASRC brought timely assistance to the Centre in its nascent stage. He helped the Centre in preparing a detailed programme and in providing the basis for architectural plans for its new building. He also set forth plans and procedures for the development of the library collection. Before his return to the U.S. in March 1967, he prepared an invaluable guide for building up the library resources of the ASRC.[72] The *programme* describes the need for a systematic acquisition practice supported by a clear book selection policy, and suggests subject areas to be covered in the order of priorities. Its importance is all the more in India where the practice of formulating clear-cut acquisition policy statements hardly exists.

In Margaret R. Russell, who had accompanied John Russell, the Centre found an experienced professional cataloguer, who worked in the ASRC library with great enthusiasm. She guided the library staff towards achieving a high standard of excellence in cataloguing.

During their stay in India, the Russells visited a number of libraries at Hyderabad, Simla, Chandigarh, New Delhi, Jaipur, Bangalore, Mysore, Waltair, Calcutta and Madras. They also participated in a number of seminars and contributed articles to several Indian journals. So far as the ASRC is concerned, it is largely because of the contribution of the Russells that it truly became an advanced centre for research in American studies.[73]

5.5.3 Jo Manning: Jo Manning visited the ASRC library for the briefest period (March 27-31, 1979) and made certain recommendations[74] towards the improvement in the procedures and practices of the Centre's library.[75]

5.5.4 Ronald and Ellen Chapman: Ronald Chapman, Librarian, Honolulu Community College, Hawaii and his wife, Ellen Chapman, Chairperson of the General Reference Division, Graduate Research Library, University of Hawaii, were contracted by the USIA (United States Information Agency) to come to the ASRC during 1984-85 primarily to evaluate its library collection, the training and competence of its staff and the efficiency of its operations with a view to suggesting improvements where necessary. The other part of their assignment was to visit all USIS libraries in India to evaluate collections, give lectures, organize workshops and make suggestions for improvement. Accordingly, in addition to their work at the ASRC, the Chapmans visited all USIS libraries in the country, some other libraries in the areas and delivered lectures to library science faculty and students. Among the lectures that Ellen Chapman gave at different places in the country, those on data-base searching need special mention.[76]

In brief, it can be said that so far as the set-up, procedures, functions and services to readers by the ASRC are concerned, the impact of the work of all these specialists who worked there has made the Centre "user-oriented" in the true sense of the term.

5.6 College of Engineering, Guindy

Eugene deBenko from the Michigan State University Library visited India for six weeks (September 2 to October 12) in 1963 to work as a short-term consultant at the Guindy College of Engineering near Madras. During this short span of time, except for a two-day visit to the Poona College of Engineering at Pune (October 2-3), deBenko spent the entire period at Guindy.

During his stay at Guindy, deBenko helped the college library develop in numerous ways. He assisted in streamlining the acquisition programme by establishing links with other foreign libraries and soliciting exchanges and gifts. As he states:

> In the collection development area, a program was commenced with technical libraries abroad (chiefly U. K. and U.S.A. libraries) to exchange Indian technical periodicals for those published abroad. This, then, helped the acquisition of foreign technical periodicals, books, technical standards, etc., without requiring foreign exchange. The college library also took advantage of the UNESCO offerings of free publications and of the services of the U.S. Book Exchange. . . . The engineering teaching/research faculty at Michigan State University also donated a large number of books and backfiles of engineering periodicals. . . to the Guindy College Library.[77]

deBenko improved reference services, recommended the acquisition of needed equipment and furniture such as telephone in the library, storage/shelving facilities for maps and atlases, book trolleys, special stands for dictionaries and thesauri, sloping shelves/racks for current issues of periodicals etc. He also helped in the physical reorganization of the library. Alongwith V. Ramachandran, the College Librarian, deBenko prepared the necessary proposal for the construction of a new building, appointment of additional staff and reorganization of library services on modern lines. The proposals were approved by the authorities and the library services were reorganized on the lines suggested by deBenko.[78] What more could have been achieved within a short span of six weeks ?

6. SPECIALISTS AT AGRICULTURAL INSTITUTIONS

Seven American library specialists came to India either to work in or to provide expertise to libraries attached to agricultural universities or agricultural research institutes. To name them chronologically, Ralph R. Shaw, Professor of Scientific Management and Library Science at Rutgers University, came in 1956; Dorothy M. Parker and Angelina Carabelli and Ning Yu Li came as chairperson and members respectively of the Indo-American Agricultural Survey Team in 1967; Don W. Jett came in 1968 to work as a specialist in Mysore Agricultural University at Bangalore; and finally, Hilary D. Burton and Trudy Brekelbaurn came to International Crops Research Institute for the Semi-Arid Tropics (ICRISAT), Hyderabad, in 1983. All except Burton and Brekelbaurn submitted their reports.

6.1 Ralph R. Shaw

Since the Indo-American Team on Agricultural Research and Education had recommended that agricultural library services needed to be improved, the Indian Council of Agricultural Research (ICAR) requested the services of Ralph R. Shaw to study the working of agricultural libraries in India and to formulate recommendations for their improvement. From the very inception of this work, Shaw was assisted at every stage by D. B. Krishna Rao, Librarian of the ICAR. The two-member team visited Nagpur, Hyderabad, Bangalore, Coimbatore, Madras, Calcutta, Anand and New Delhi to study and observe the libraries working in twenty different institutions including agricultural colleges, universities, veterinary colleges and agricultural research institutes at these places.

Shaw and his colleague submitted their *Report*[79] which contained twenty recommendations of considerable value and added to the effectiveness of libraries in agricultural teaching and research. The main thrust of their recommendations was for ICAR to become a national bibliographical and library service agency and also to prepare a basic list of books and periodicals for each course of instruction in the agricultural and veterinary colleges. Recognising the inadequacies of financial resources available to the libraries of agricultural and veterinary colleges and other institutions in India, they outlined the role that could be placed by Technical Cooperation Mission and other U.S. foundations in this regard and suggested that the U.S. aid could be better utilized for developing collections and improving services of the libraries at these institutions. Unfortunately, "many of the Shaw-Krishna Rao recommendations were not put into effect because of the lack of an organization which could provide continuing direction, co-ordination, administration and financing for a library programme".[80]

6.2 Dorothy M. Parker, Ming Yu Li and Angelina Carabelli

Developments in the new agricultural research institutes and universities in India during 1960s created new pressures for the improvement of libraries serving the needs of agricultural research, education and extension. At the request of the directors of different institutes of ICAR, it was agreed, in May 1967, to sponsor a review of existing library facilities then existing. To do this, a group of American and Indian librarians, was invited to conduct a survey and make recommendations for the improvement of twenty-four libraries of the ICAR institutes and eight agricultural universities. The American members of the team were Dorothy M. Parker (Chairperson), Ming Yu Li and Angelina Carabelli and the Indian members were S. P. Phadnis (Secretary), S. R. Banerjee and D. R. Kalia.

The team paid official visits to eighteen research institutes and eight agricultural universities then in existence. Unofficial visits were paid to other libraries and documentation centres including INSDOC, Publications and Information Directorate, the National Physical Laboratory, the National Library of Medicine, New Delhi, Indian Institute of Science, Bangalore, Agricultural Colleges at Ranchi and Coimbatore, Universities of Kerala and Jodhpur and the Indian Statistical Institute, Calcutta.

The team in its *Report*[81] made sixty-nine recommendations with regard to different aspects of agricultural library services such as ICAR library and documentation programme, Indian National Agricultural Library etc. By far the most important of its recommendation urged the establishment of an Indian National Agricultural Library to give leadership and direction to agricultural libraries in India.

6.3 Don W. Jett

Don W. Jett visited the Mysore University of Agricultural Science at Bangalore in 1968 and submitted a brief report[82] to the University, providing the history and background of the University Library, its objectives, building, collection, book selection policy, acquisition, processing, reader services, staff and budget. He made six recommendations concerning staff, card catalogue project, circulation procedures, book procurement aids, buildings and equipment and library development in general.

6.4 Hilary D. Burton and Trudy Brekelbaurn

A two-member Sorghum and Millet Information Centre[83] evaluation team, consisting of Hilary D. Burton, Technical Information Specialist, USDA Agricultural Research Service and Trudy Brekelbaurn, Texas A & M University, College Station, visited SMIC and the ICRISAT Library and Documentation Services at Hyderabad, during 18 May to 2 June 1983. They met with a representative cross-section of the ICRISAT scientists as well as other Indian scientists to elicit their views about the SMIC services.[84] As stated earlier, they did not submit any formal report.

7. SPECIALISTS WITH SHORT-TERM ASSIGNMENTS

Three American library specialists viz. Sarah K. Vann, Henry Scholberg and James E. Agenbroad, visited India with some short-term assignments. Vann came in 1964 and Agenbroad in 1982, whereas Scholberg visited India a number of times during 1964-85.

7.1 Sarah K. Vann

On behalf of the American Library Association, Sarah K. Vann visited India, among other countries, as Director of the Field Survey of the Dewey Decimal Classification (DDC) use abroad. At the time of Dewey's death in 1931, DDC was used barely in twenty countries, but just thirty years later it was being used in more than one hundred countries. Because of the widespread use of DDC, a field survey which was conducted jointly by Sarah K. Vann and Pauline A. Seely in 1964 was undertaken to test its strengths and weaknesses.[85] Vann's circuit included India. Some of the observations made by her in connection with the use of DDC in India are worth mentioning. She wrote:

> That India is the largest user of DDC in the Orient might reflect its early introduction into the Indo/Pakistan Subcontinent. It was in 1915 that Asa Don Dickinson first used Dewey at the Panjab University in Lahore. . . . An extract, with expansions appropriate to Indian topics, has been prepared in Bengali by S. Mookerjee of the University of Calcutta. In 1964, the Indian Library Association

passed a resolution that the Association assume responsibility for translations into twelve Indian languages, among them Hindi and Tamil.[86]

How extensively DDC is used in India would not have been clear but for Vann's survey.

7.2 Henry Scholberg

During the years 1964-85, Henry Scholberg visited India as many as eight times in connection with research projects, for acquisition of books and for attending seminars. During his first visit in 1964, Scholberg conducted research on his first book *The District Gazetteers of British India–A bibliography*.[87] His second visit to India was a book-buying expedition. He further visited India in 1975, 1976 and 1979 to conduct research on and prepare the final draft of his book *Bibliography of Goa and the Protuguese in India*, which was published in 1982.

Subsequently, Scholberg visited India twice to attend seminars. In 1979, he attended a library seminar in Jaipur, organized by N. N. Gidwani, and in 1983, he attended the third international seminar on Indo-Portuguese History in Goa. In 1983, he also carried out research for his book *The Encyclopedias of India*.[88] His visit in 1985 was for a photographic survey of the forts of Portuguese India.[89]

7.3 James E. Agenbroad

James E. Agenbroad, Systems Analyst in the Library of Congress, visited India twice–in June 1980 for a week to establish professional contacts and again in 1982 for about three months in connection with his research project on survey of computer processing of Indian languages. The project had two goals, viz. to understand and report the status in late 1982 of computer processing of Indian alphabets and to bring the recent impact of computer on American libraries to the attention of Indians so that they could assess its relevance to their needs. In this connection, he visited the Tata Institute of Fundamental Research, Bombay; National Informatics Centre, Delhi and Indian Institute of Technology, Kanpur.[90]

8. SPECIALISTS AS DELEGATES TO SEMINARS/CONFERENCES

No American library specialist visited India as a delegate to a seminar or conference prior to 1975, except Jay E. Daily of the Pittsburgh University who attended the Unesco seminar in Delhi in October 1960. However, during the 1970s and 1980s, a few American library specialists visited India to attend seminars/conferences. These seminars/conferences were the Third International Study Conference on Classification Research, held at Bombay in 1975 and the Indo-US seminars on scientific and technical information, held at Bangalore and Delhi in 1977 and 1980 respectively.

8.1 American Delegates to the Third International Study Conference on Classification Research

The first instance of American delegates attending any library conference in India on a large scale was the Third International Study Conference on Classification Research held at Bombay during 6-11 January, 1975. Among the eleven delegates from the U.S. were Pauline A. Atherton, Harold Borko, Eugene Garfield, David F. Hersey, J. P. Immroth, F. W. Lancaster, Christine A. Montgomery, Malcolm Rigby, J. H. Schneider, J. R. R. Dere-Mountague and R. N. Paul. Except the last two, who attended the conference as observers, others presented papers which are published in the proceedings of the Conference.[91]

8.2 American Delegates to the Indo-US Seminar on Scientific and Technical Information

A large number of American delegates attended the Indo-US seminars on scientific and technical information, organized by the Indo-US Sub-Commission on Science and Technology. Of the three seminars organized by the Sub-Commission so far, the first was held at Washington (D. C.) in 1976, whereas the remaining two took place in India at Bangalore and Delhi in 1977 and 1980 respectively.

8.2.1 American Delegates to the Second Indo-US Seminar : The second Indo-US Seminar, held at Bangalore during 18-22 July, 1977 to discuss "Information science education" and "User education", was co-chaired by A. Neelameghan, Head, DRTC, and Carole A. Ganz, Program Associate, Division of Information, Science and Technology, National Science Foundation, Washington (D.C.). Of the nine American delegates who attended the seminar, only five presented papers. Ganz presented his paper on "Education and training–for the user and for the information scientists"; Vladmir Slamecka on "Resource planning for the library/information science school;" and

Donald J. Hillman on "A training program in energy information systems". Papers on "Hands on on-line in multi-system, multi-data base trainer" and "Information education in the engineering class room" were presented by Elaine Caruso and B. G. Barr respectively.[92] The other American delegates who attended the seminar were Neil Haley, Mary Agnes Ruffier, David Floyd Hersey and Joseph G. Gratton.

8.2.2 American Delegates to the Third Indo-US Seminar: The third Indo-US seminar, designated as "workshop", on "Scientific and technological information" was organized at Delhi during 10-12 March, 1980 and was attended by seven American delegates, all of whom presented papers. Pranas Zunde presented two papers, the first on "Modelling national science and technology information systems–problems and prospects"; and the second, jointly with V. Venkata Rao on the "Technique of modelling large-scale scientific and technical information systems". William R. Nugent's paper was on "The information-intensive community" and that of Marshall C. Yovits on "A generalized model for establishing performances and evaluation criteria for information systems". The theme of Vernon E. Palmour's paper was "Describing national scientific and technical information systems–macro and micro models" and Donald J. Hillman in his paper provided "A simulation model of the online information retrieval system of the National Library of Medicine". The remaining two papers on "Future research directions in the economic analysis of information systems", and "National information systems–implications of new and anticipated technology advances" were presented by Michael D. Cooper and H. L. Resnikoff respectively.[93]

8.3 American Delegates to the International Conference on Ranganathan's Philosophy

Regrettably, no American delegate attended the International conference on Ranganathan's philosophy which was organized at Delhi during 11-14 November, 1985 under the joint auspices of the Indian Library Association and the Sarada Ranganathan Endowment for Library Science. F. W. Lancaster's lone paper was read *in absentia* and is included in the Conference Proceedings.[94]

9. OTHER SPECIALISTS

In addition to the American library specialists discussed above, a few more should be taken note of. Some came with their own projects for extended periods, others for a few weeks and still others just to visit India and her libraries. Prominent among these specialists were Maureen L. P. Patterson, Keyes D. Metcalf, John F. Harvey, F. W. Lancaster, Paul Wasserman, Miles M. Jackson, Quincy Mumford, Daniel J. Boorstin, Jack Dalton, R. C. Swank, Lester Asheim and Luther H. Evans. Their visits to and work in India is discussed below.

9.1 Maureen L. P. Patterson

Maureen Patterson, Bibliographer and Head, South Asia Collection at the University of Chicago, and also Associate Professor in the Department of South Asian Languages and Civilization in the same University, has been associated with India in more than one capacity since 1944-46, when she was stationed in Delhi with the U.S. Army as part of war effort against the Japanese. She was so inspired by the Indian ethos that it did not take her long to decide that she would make India her academic focus, and to that end, she assiduously studied Indian languages such as Hindi, Sanskrit and Marathi. Her second visit to India (1953-55) was in pursuance of her research for her post-graduate work at the University of Pennsylvania.[95] She spent these years at Pune. Both these visits reinforced her interest in India, Indian languages and Indian social reforms. During her third visit in 1982, she toured extensively in Maharashtra, as she wanted to explore the place of *Chitpavanas* (a Brahmin sub-caste) in Maharashtra's social history over the past three hundred years.

Among her publications, those of professional interest to librarians are *South Asia: An Introductory Bibliography on South Asia* (Chicago, 1962), *South Asian Library Resources in North America*, in two volumes (Zug, Switzerland, 1975) and *South Asian Civilization: A Bibliographic Synthesis* (Chicago, 1981). But her major literary output consists of a number of socio-economic articles on Maharashtra published in the Economic Weekly, *Encyclopedia Americanna* and Singer and Cohn's volume on *Structure and Change in Indian Society*. In recognition of her extensive knowledge of literature concerning South Asia, she was entrusted with the supervision of the building of the South Asia collection in the University of Chicago and was invited by the Library of Congress to advise on its South Asia Book Procurement Program since its inception in 1962.

Patterson's contribution to India can best be summed up in her own words when she states, ". . . all my work is aimed at developing among

Americans a better understanding of the long-lived and the distinguished civilization of the sub-continent, one of the world's most ancient and persistent. Americans can no longer remain in ignorance of the land and people of nearly one-fifth of the entire globe".[96]

9.2 Keyes D. Metcalf

Keyes D. Metcalf, retired Director of Harvard University Library and formerly Director of the New York Public Library, visited India in 1959 on behalf of the Rockefeller Foundation. He is considered one of the foremost authorities on library planning in the U.S. and also had had extensive practical experience in the organization and operation of library facilities. When he visited a number of Asian countries in 1959, he was mainly engaged in planning new libraries. He visited India for six weeks (February-March 1959) as a consultant to assist with the plans for the libraries at the Indian Agricultural Research Institute and the All India Institute of Medical Sciences.[97] Despite his short stay in India, he managed visits to Delhi, Calcutta and Bombay.

At Delhi, Metcalf met S. R. Ranganathan and had extended discussions with him regarding standards for planning of library buildings, particularly university library buildings. He attended two sessions of a four-day seminar on university library problems–first of its kind ever held in India–and spoke on some basic problems of university libraries. He also delivered two talks at the Delhi Library Association and visited the Dyal Singh Library in Delhi.[98]

While at Calcutta where he could spend only one week, Metcalf visited the National Library and discussed its problems with the librarian, B. S. Kesavan. Kesavan took the opportunity also to obtain his comments on the report on library development, prepared by a committee which included Kesavan himself.[99] On his return trip to Delhi, Metcalf spent a couple of days at Bombay where he had talks with the librarians of the University of Bombay, the Archives, the Asiatic Society and a few other libraries.[100]

Easily, the most important of Metcalf's recommendations can be said to be that local public library service in towns and villages. should be closely connected with schools and with the social welfare and social education groups in order to prevent unnecessary duplication of services.[101] As he puts it,

> "If new schools are built which are fairly large in size and serve a considerable population, it should be possible to have one room in

> the school building that can be used as a school library, a social education center, and also a public library. It should also be possible to reduce buildings costs in this way and also to reduce the need for a large number of persons to provide library service. . . . These combined school and public libraries be part of a district library system and that the book collections be shifted from one school to another at frequent intervals".[102]

It is unfortunate that Metcalf's eminently practical suggestion did not receive due consideration either of the Government or of the managements running schools or public libraries in India.

9.3 John F. Harvey

John F. Harvey, Dean of Library Services, University of New Mexico, undertook a seven-week trip to visit libraries in twelve countries including India, West Asia, and the Soviet Union in the summer of 1970. In India, he visited twenty-five libraries situated at Delhi, Hyderabad and Bombay, such as libraries attached to American Studies Research Centre, Osmania University (both at Hyderabad), Tata Institute of Fundamental Research, Royal Asiatic Society, British Council Library, American Center Library, SNDT Women's University and University of Bombay (all at Bombay). Accounts of his visits to libraries in Hyderabad and Bombay have been published in Indian Journals.[103-104] What is important from an Indian point of view, is Harvey's observation of Indian librarianship, which reads as:

> Often Indian university libraries had good-sized book collections but did not exploit free and exchange possibilities sufficiently, nor were they always led by vigorous, public-spirited administrators. Obvious, government-supported public librarianship was just beginning and was unable to obtain a high-budget priority. Apparently, many useful special libraries had been established, and information science had achieved a good start in Delhi and Bangalore. School libraries seemed to be poor, though doubtless a few exceptional school libraries existed, like the one at American International School. Library schools were fortunate enough to teach in English but suffered from their small size and prestige and with their fascination for cataloguing. Library associations seemed to be numerous, small, contentious, and professionally ineffective. The poorly paid librarians themselves seemed wary and nervous, in

some ways sensitive, in other ways insensitive, the quality of life affecting their behavior, the quality of bureaucratic red tape affecting their success.[105]

There is much to be learnt from Harvey's observations by Indian librarians and also by those who are one way or other concerned with librarianship in India.

9.4 F. W. Lancaster

F. W. Lancaster, Professor at the Graduate School of Library and Information Science, University of Illinois, visited India twice–in 1980 and in 1985. During his first visit which was sponsored by the U.S. Embassy in India, he was the principal lecturer at two conferences on Entering the Information Age, held at Bangalore and Pune. In these conferences, he presented his views regarding the future of publishing, libraries and information transfer in general. He also visited Madras, Bombay and Delhi.[106] During his second visit to India in November 1985, he was the resource person in the Asian Regional seminar/workshop on thesaurus construction, organized by INSDOC at Delhi from November 18 to 29.

9.5 Paul Wasserman

Paul Wasserman visited India twice, in January 1981 and again in 1987. During his first visit, he served as a Unesco Consultant directing a two-week management workshop sponsored by Unesco in Delhi at India International Centre. The workshop programme was modelled after the Library Administrative Development Program offered at the University of Maryland annually. The participants included library and information managers drawn from India and the surrounding region including Afghanistan, Siberia, Indonesia, Pakistan, Iran and two or three other countries. Wasserman prepared programme plan and made general arrangements. He served as the Resident-Director and delivered lectures in some of the areas including decision-making in libraries, the librarian as manager of a complex organization etc.[107]

During his second visit to India during April 1989 for about a fortnight, Wasserman delivered talks at library schools in the Universities of Delhi and Poona and was the resource person in a two-day seminar on management issues and trends in library and information science, organized by the Panjab University Library, Chandigarh, in collaboration with the American Center, New Delhi.

9.6 Miles M. Jackson

Miles M. Jackson, Dean of Library Science at the University of Hawaii, Honolulu, had been to India for about a month during November-December 1983 and visited Delhi, Calcutta, Bangalore, Mysore, Hyderabad and Bombay. He was the resource-person at the seminars organized by the USIS libraries at all the four centres in India, viz. Bombay, Calcutta, Delhi and Madras. He visited the National Library and the Indian Institute of Management (both at Calcutta); attended the 29th All India Library Conference, organized by the Indian Library Association at Mysore and delivered the keynote address; also attended seminars organized by the Documentation Research and Training Centre (Bangalore) and the American Studies Research Centre (Hyderabad).

During his stay in India, Jackson met with high level librarians and information scientists from the Government of India, universities and specialized information centres, who were involved in discussions on the free flow of information, information sharing, and forging useful links between American and Indian institutions.[108]

9.7 Quincy Mumford and Daniel J. Boorstin

Quincy Mumford and Daniel J. Boorstin, both Librarians, Library of Congress, paid short visits to India in November 1963 and January 1984 respectively. At the reception accorded to him by Charles John Finzi, Director, Library of Congress Book Procurement Centre, Delhi, Mumford stated that there was a growing urge in the U.S. to know "more and more about India".[109]

Daniel J. Boorstin (with Mrs. Boorstin) visited India in January 1984 at the invitation of the Indian Council of Cultural Relations. During his visit, Boorstin reviewed the operations of the Library of Congress field office, Delhi, and discussed with E. Gene Smith, Field Director, the work of processing books for the Library of Congress. He called upon Prime Minister Indira Gandhi. Boorstin also visited Varanasi, Calcutta, Madras and Bombay, meeting distinguished scholars, journalists and scientists. At Calcutta, he attended the bicentennial celebrations of the Asiatic Society.[110]

9.8 Jack Dalton, R. C. Swank and Lester Asheim

Jack Dalton, R. C. Swank and Lester Asheim visited India in the capacity of Directors of the International Relations Office in the ALA. Dalton visited India for four times, twice in 1957, and once each in

1958 and 1959; Swank only once during October-December 1960 and Asheim twice–once during March-May 1963 and during December 1963-March 1964 for the second time.

At the time of both of his trips to India, Asheim was Director of the International Relations Office in the ALA, and in that capacity, one of his responsibilities was to visit different countries of the world to observe developments in library services and education for librarianship, with a view to identifying needs and interests to which American librarians and agencies might make some constructive contributions.[111] In both these trips, he visited many places–Delhi, Jaipur, Agra, Aligarh, Lucknow, Varanasi, Calcutta, Madras, Bangalore, Hyderabad, Bombay, Baroda and Pune–and talked to several librarians and educators about their concerns and was helpful in identifying American specialists who could act as more direct and intensive consultants.[112]

9.9 Luther H. Evans

Luther H. Evans visited India thrice–in 1951, 1954 and 1956. When he visited India for the first time during November-December 1951, he was with the Columbia University. His later visits were not in any way related to library field, but were undertaken in his capacity as the Director-General of Unesco. During his first visit to India, Evans gave a talk on Libraries and Unesco to students of library science at the University of Delhi.[113] That was a topic that must have been dear to his heart, for Evans had abiding affection for libraries as well as Unesco, stemming as it did from his association with the Library of Congress as its Librarian (1945-53) and with Unesco first as Chief of the U.S. Mission (1952-53) and then as Unesco's Director-General (1953-58). He delivered a similar talk at a meeting of librarians in the Central Secretariat Library and an address on "the importance of archival work in building up a strong democratic state" to the staff of the National Archives of India.[114]

9.9.1 A Few More Names also Deserve Mention: For example, Avila A. Pelletier, Head of the Publications Section of the Technical Information Division in the Library of Congress, had been in India from November 1952 to December 1955. During this period, he worked in the INSDOC as a Unesco expert in the framework of a UN Technical Assistance Project as a Mechanical Processing Specialist. His task was "to organize and supervise reproduction services including photostats, microfilms, microcards and near printing processes".[115] So also, David T. Ray, a scholar in Indian scripts and languages, while working as a cataloguer in the Morris Library, University of Illinois, visited India during 1962-63. Though he was primarily interested in the study of Indian scripts and languages, he spent some time in visiting twenty-two libraries situated at Trivandrum, Madras, Bangalore, Bombay, Calcutta, Patna and Varanasi.[116] The *Directory*, mentioned earlier, includes names of H. Tyler Gemmell, Helen E. Wessells, Alan L. Heyneman, Raymond P. Morris and Paul Bixler. Gemmell worked as a library consultant at the Isabella Thoburn College, Lucknow, for one term during 1966-67 under the US-India's Women's College Exchange Program, whereas others paid visits to India during the 1950s and early 1960s.

9.9.2 Antoinette Strobino, Malcolm M. Willey and J. Arthur Branch and Welthy H. Fisher: The account of the contribution of the American library specialist to libraries and librarianship in India will be somewhat incomplete without passingly mentioning the work of Antoinette Strobino, Malcolm M. Willey and J. Arthur Branch and Wealthy H. Fisher, though they did not belong to the library profession. So also, William Webb, and Richard Greenfield, Information Specialist, Library of Congress visited India during 1987 and 1988 respectively.

9.9.2.1 Antoinette Strobino: Antoinette Strobino, an American Peace volunteer, came to Walajabad, a small town in Chingleput District of Tamil Nadu, sometime in 1971, to teach English and hygiene at the Government Basic Training School. Not content with just teaching, she sought other ways to help "her" village. When she suggested to the people of the village the idea of starting a library for children, they immediately donated land for the building. Books began to come in even before the building went up. Then help came from the U.S. The students of Belding School in Belding, Michigan, raised Rs. 11,400 toward putting up the building. Today, the library has a collection of thousands of books in English and hundreds in Tamil. Many American publishers and individuals sent book to Chingleput. The library is a "youth memorial" to Strobino's service to India.[117]

9.9.2.2 Malcolm M. Willey and J. Arthur Branch: Malcolm M. Willey, Consultant on higher education and J. Arthur Branch, consultant on business organization and administration, visited India, on behalf of the Ford Foundation, during the 1960s and prepared A Self Study Manual for Indian Universities and Colleges.[118] What is significant for the present study is that the Manual contains a chapter on university library, posing several questions rregarding library resources, use of the library by teachers and students and organization and administration of the library. The chapter in the form of discussion-guide is of great help for the smooth and efficient running of academic libraries and their evaluation.

9.9.2.3 Welthy Honsinger Fisher: A native of Rome N. Y., Welthy Honsinger learned to love India since 1924, when she married Frederick B. Fisher, Methodist Bishop of Calcutta and Burma, and in so doing, "married India". After the death of her husband, Fisher visited India in 1939. During her next visit in 1947 she met Mahatama Gandhi who told her "when you come back to live in India, go to the villages and help them. India is the villages". She came to India four years after, to start a new life at the age of 72 and founded in 1953 the Literacy House at Lucknow,[119] which has played a significant role in Indian librarianship.

In the initial stages of it, the bell-bicycle librarians of the Literacy House visited remote villages in Lucknow district to serve regularly the inhabitants of these villages with the booklets of specially prepared reading material for neoliterates, both grown-ups and children.[120]

The Literacy House now runs six types of library services viz. market mobile libraries, halting mobile libraries, workers' mobile libraries, bell-bicycle-libraries, district deposit library centres and library kits for literacy classes. Over and above this network, the Literacy House has a library on its campus. The campus library has given a big boost to the literacy movement in India, as well as in other Asian countries, not only by expanding the professional horizons of the staff of the Literacy House, but also by its active outreach to feed vital information and provide services to other researchers in the same field.[121]

In the rightness of things, instead of speaking about three R's, Fisher could speak of four F's–Functional literacy, Family planning, Food production and Freedom to choose one's own government[122]-which are vital to rural India. Recipient of several national and international honorary degrees and awards, such as Ramon Magasaysay Award, Nehru Literacy Award, Humanitarian

Award of the Variety Clubs International of the U.S., Fisher has been described by President Zakir Hussain as 'a national institution'. She lit a candle so that the world could learn.

10. SUMMARY

The above account of the contribution of American library specialists to Indian libraries and librarianship, during the past seventy odd years, reveals the extent to which the U.S. has helped Indian librarianship to develop. The specialists came to India in various capacities as library directors, librarians, advisers, lecturers or on some other assignments. They travelled to various parts of the country and worked in universities and libraries attached to varied institutions. Some stayed here comparatively for a longer period–as much as a couple of years–whereas some others came more often than just once. There can be no doubt that their work and expertise has immensely enriched Indian librarianship.

During the past few years, facilities for library science education have made rapid strides in India, and the consequent availability of highly qualified Indians has persuaded the USIS authorities to appoint Indians as library directors in the American Centers in different parts of the country, instead of inviting American specialists to occupy those positions. This has naturally resulted in a gradual dwindling of the number of American library specialists coming out to India on assignments. Fortunately, however, because of the establishment of the Indo-US Joint Commission, American library specialists have continued to take interest in Indian librarianship, and hopefully, their expertise would not cease to be available to India in the years to come. Their assistance, at this stage, would be especially welcome in the field of the application of computer and telecommunication technology in the provision of library and information service. In view of their invaluable assistance over the past many years as described above, it would be in the fitness of things if the U.S. leads India across the threshold of the new technological revolution.

NOTES AND REFERENCES

1. Janet C. Phillips, *Foreign Service Directory of American Librarians*, Pittsburgh, 1967, p. xiii.

2. Hall B. Schell, "Library consultants and consulting," in *Encyclopedia of Library and Information Science*, Vol. 15, New York, 1975, pp. 201-14.
3. J. Stephen Parker, "The overseas library consultant," *Library Review*. 28 (1979): 214-25.
4. L. F. Stieg, "American librarians abroad—1946-65," *Library Quarterly*, 38 (1968): 315-22.
5. A. C. Hansen, "Gold in the foreign service roster", *A. L. A. Bulletin*, 39 (1945): 14-17.
6. M. M., Amin, "The library movement in Charotar mitra mandal libraries—the first library movement," *Modern Librarian*, 7 (1936-37): 30-38.
7. In some cases, there is overlap of periods. For example, Beatrice Holt (as an adviser) was in india from 1955 to 1961. For the sake of convenience, in categorising such cases, the year in which the specialist came to India is taken into account. So also, some specialists visited India more than once. For example, Jennings Wood visited India twice—during 1958-59 and again in 1961-62. For the sake of convenience, in categorising such cases, the year/s in which the specialists visited India for the first time is/are taken into account. His/Her subsequent visit/s is/are not counted, though described.
8. D. R. Kalia and J. C. Mehta, "The impact of recent developments on Indian libraries," in *International Librarianship*, London, 1972, pp. 49-53.
9. N. C. Chakravarty, "Lest we forget-pioneers who are no more," *I. L. A. Bulletin*, 3 (1967): 96-103.
10. W. A. Borden, "Baroda, India, and its libraries," *Library Journal*, 38 (1913): 659-63.
11. *Ibid.*
12. *Ibid.*
13. Kalia and Mehta, *op. cit.*
14. S. R. Bhatia, "History of libraries and the library movement in the Punjab" *Modern Librarian*, 6 (1935-36): 87-97.
15. Labhu Ram, "Principal Woolner's dream or the phenomenal growth of the Panjab University Library," *Modern Librarian*, 4 (1933-34): 41-53.
16. *Ibid.*
17. *Ibid.*
18. *Ibid.*
19. Published by the Panjab University Library, Lahore, 1916, pp. 242.
20. *Ibid.*
21. "The library movement in the Punjab—paper submitted by the Library Association, Lahore, to the All Asia Educational Conference held at Benares on December 26-30, 1930, *Modern Librarian*, 1 (1930-31): 55-58.
22. A. D. Dickinson, *Panjab Library Primer*, Lahore, 1916.
23. "The library movement in the Punjab," *op. cit.*
24. Flora B. Ludhington, "The American contribution to foreign library establishment and rehabilitation," *Library Quarterly*, 24 (1954): 192-204.
25. Katharine S. Diehl, "Books and common education in the Indo-Pak sub-continent 1959-1962," *Journal of Library History*, 2 (1967): 201-10.
26. Details have been provided by Dr. B. Anderson, Bombay.
27. Howard W. Winger, "Aspects of librarianship: a trace work of history," *Library Quarterly*, 31, (1961): 321-35.

28. Beverly J. Brewster, *American Overseas Library Technical Assistance, 1940-1970*, Metuchen (N. J.), 1976, p. 40.
29. B. S. Kesavan, *India's National Library*, Calcutta, 1961, p. 42.
30. John Alden, *Report to Mr. B. S. Kesavan, Librarian, National Library*, Calcutta, 8 May 1958, *Typescript*.
31. K. S. Deshpande, "The Wheat Loan Programme and its impact on the Indian library world," *Granthapal*, 4 (1962): 118-25.
32. "Academic and research libraries in India," *College and Research Libraries*, 20 (1959): 243-46.
33. Laurence J. Kipp and Cecilia Rae Kipp, *Indian Libraries and the India Wheat Loan Educational Exchange Program — A Report*, Mimeographed, 1961.
34. H. C. Jain, "Achievements of academic libraries in India—A decennial review," *Library Herald*, 6 (1963-64): 172-80.
35. Kipp and Kipp, *op. cit.*
36. A. K. Mukherjee, "Wheat Loan Educational Exchange Programme in India and the Indian university libraries," *Library Herald*, 6 (1963-64): 96-102.
37. Carl M. White, *A Survey of the University of Delhi Library*, Delhi, 1965, pp. 184.
38. *Ibid.*, p. xii.
39. *Ibid.*, pp. xiii-xvi.
40. B. S. Kesavan, "Editorial—Carl White Report," *Annals of Library Science and Documentation*, 12 (1965): 119-28.
41. Girja Kumar, "University libraries in India—A case study: A survey of the University of Delhi Library, Carl M. White, planning unit, University of Delhi," *University News*, 4 (October 1966): 17-18.
42. N. K. Goil, "Survey of the University of Delhi library by Carl M. White—A review," *Library Herald*, 8 (1965-66): 290-92.
43. H. C. Mehta, "White report," *University News*. 4 (November 1966): 16.
44. C. S. Krishnamurti, "Survey of the University of Delhi library by Carl M. White—A review," *Library Herald*, 8 (1965-66): 292-94.
45. Rudolph Gjelsness, "Review of a survey of the University of Delhi library by Carl M. White," *College and Research Libraries*, 27 (1966) ; 490-91.
46. Carl. M White's letter dated 15 February 1967 to H. C. Mehta.
47. *Ibid.*, dated 28 August 1972 to H. C. Mehta.
48. *Ibid.*
49. Malcolm M. Willey and J. Arthur Branch, *A Self-Study Manual for Indian Universities and Colleges*, Delhi, 1968, p. 37.
50. *Ibid.*
51. A. P. Srivastava in an interview on 2 May 1985.
52. Shera could not come to India for reasons of health, and his lectures were, therefore, "delivered" from pre-recorded tapes (*Sociological Foundations of Librarianship*, p. 5).
53. J. H. Shera, *Sociological Foundations of Librarianship*, Bangalore, 1970, pp. 195.
54. Pauline A. Atherton, *Putting Knowledge to Work—An American View of Ranganathan's Five Laws of Library Science*, Bangalore, 1973, pp. 158.
55. Jean M. Perreault, *The Idea of Order in Bibliography*, Bangalore, 1978, pp. 135.

56. Charles P. Bourne, *Technology in Support of Library Science and Information Service*, Bangalore, 1980, pp. 78.
57. "Notes and news," *Herald of Library Science*, 10 (1971): 188.
58. National Information System in Science and Technology in India, a national plan which emerged from Dr. Peter Lazar's recommendations made to the Council of Scientific and Industrial Research, Government of India, to develop an information system on technology.
59. Jean M. Perreault's letter dated 26 March 1984 to the author.
60. All these details have been collected from the enclosures to Charles P. Bourne's letter dated 17 May 1984 to the author.
61. *Ibid.*
62. P. A. Mohanrajan, ed., *New Trends in International Librarianship—S. R. Ranganathan Festschrift to mark the Platinum of Madras University Library*, New Delhi, 1984, pp. 263-79.
63. All these lectures have been published in *Library Science* with a Slant to Documentation.
64. All these details have been taken from Patrick R. Penland's letter dated 28 March 1984 to the author.
65. *Ibid.*
66. *IASLIC Newsletter*, April 1985, p. 2.
67. Indian Institute of Technology, Kanpur, *Annual Report 1961-62*, pp. 16-17.
68. *Ibid. Annual Report 1962-63*, p. 5.
69. Brewster, *op. cit.*, p. 58.
70. Indian Institute of Technology, Kanpur, *Annual Report 1968-69*, p. 139.
71. The details have been collected from the ASRC's newsletter *The Month at ASRC*, July 1979, pp. 1-2.
72. *An Acquisition Program for the Library of ASRC*, March 1967, Mimeographed.
73. American Studies Research Centre, Hyderabad, *Newsletter*, No. 11 (December 1967): 19-20.
74. *Library Evaluation*, 1979, Mimeographed.
75. The details have been collected from the ASRC's newsletter *The Month at ASRC*, March 1979.
76. Ronald Chapman in an interview on 5 September 1985.
77. Eugene deBenko's letter dated 2 August 1985 to the author.
78. College of Engineering, Guindy's letter dated 26 September 1984 to the author.
79. Ralph R. Shaw and D. B. Krishna Rao, *Report on Library and Bibliographical Services for Agricultural Teaching and Research in India*, New Delhi, 1957, pp. 59.
80. Dorothy Parker *et al.*, *Final Report on the ICAR Institutes and Agricultural University Libraries*, New Delhi, 1969, p. iv.
81. *Ibid.*
82. Don W. Jett, *Mysore University of Agricultural Science—Library Development Consultant Report*, Mimeographed.
83. This is part of ICRISAT Library and Documentation Services. The International Development Research Centre is financing the SMIC project for collection of world literature on these two crops, i. e. Sorghum (Jowar) and millet (Bajara).

84. The details have been collected from the enclosures to the letter from ICRISAT, Hyderabad, dated 24 July 1984 to the author.
85. Sarah K. Vann, "Dewey abroad the field survey of 1964," *Library Resources and Technical Services*, 11 (1967): 61-71.
86. *Ibid.*
87. Published by Inter Documentation Company, Zug, Switzerland, in 1970.
88. Published by Promilla & Co., New Delhi, 1986, pp. 109.
89. All these details have been collected from Henry Scholberg's letter dated 20 March 1984 to the author.
90. Data have been collected from James E. Agenbroad's research proposal, Mimeographed.
91. A. Neelameghan, ed., *Ordering Systems for Global Information Networks: Proceedings of the Third International Study Conference on Classification Research held at Bombay, India, During 6-11 January 1975*, Bangalore, 1979, pp. 511.
92. All these papers, alongwith those presented by the Indian participants, have been published in *Library Science with a Slant to Documentation*, 15 (1978), pp. 206.
93. These papers, alongwith those presented by the Indian participants, have been published in the *Workshop proceedings—Third Indo-US Workshop on Scientific and Technological Information*, 10-12 March 1980, Delhi, 1980, pp. 157.
94. F. W. Lancaster, "The library as a growing organism," in *Ranganathan's Philosophy—Assessment, Impact and Relevance—Proceedings of the International Conference Organized by the Indian Library Association and co-sponsored by Sarada Ranganathan Endowment for Library Science*, Delhi, 1986, pp. 51-53.
95. The topic of her research was *Brahman-Brahmanetarvad* (Brahmin non-Brahmin conflict)
96. All these data have been collected from the *Bio-data* provided by Maureen L. P. Patterson during her visit to Pune in 1982.
97. Rockefeller Foundation, "Appointment of Dr. Keyes Metcalf as Special Temporary Scientific Aide," Official document, 5 September 1958.
98. Keyes D. Metcalf's letter dated 19 March 1959 to the Rockefeller Foundation.
99. *Ibid.*, to B. S. Kesavan.
100. *Ibid.*
101. *Ibid.*
102. *Ibid.*
103. John F. Harvey, "Libraries in Hyderabad," *Herald of Library Science*, 13 (1974): 125-35.
104. John F. Harvey, "Libraries in Bombay," *Indian Librarian*, 28 (1973-74): 129-36.
105. *Ibid.*
106. F. W. Lancaster's letter dated 27 September 1984 to the author.
107. Paul Wasserman's letter dated 1 May 1984 to the author.
108. Details have been provided by the USIS, Delhi.
109. "Notes and news," *Herald of Library Science*, 3 (1964): 78.
110. Staff news," *Library of Congress Information Bulletin* 43 (11), 12 March 1984.
111. Lester Asheim's letter dated 30 March 1984 to the author.

112. *Ibid.*
113. Data have been collected from the enclosures to Unesco's letter dated 4 May 1984 to the author.
114. *Ibid.*
115. *Ibid.*
116. "Notes and news," *Herald of Library Science*, 2 (1963): 265.
117. S. Diwakar, "Memorial to a young lady's efforts," *American Reporter*, 23 (10 January 1973): 8.
118. Please see reference No. 49.
119. *Literacy and Development: A Commemorative Volume for Welthy Honsinger Fisher*, Delhi, 1973, p. 9.
120. T. Drieberg, "The man with the tin trunk," *Indian Journal of Adult Education*, 40 (September 1979): 41-43.
121. *Ibid.*
122. *Literacy and Development*, *op. cit.*, p. 10.

3

U.S. ROLE IN LIBRARY COLLECTION DEVELOPMENT IN INDIA

1. INTRODUCTION

As discussed in the previous chapter, quite a large number of American specialists in the field of librarianship came to India and different institutions in the country, and Indian librarianship as a whole, greatly benefited by their work, advice and expertise. Another way how these institutions benefited was through substantial grants from the U.S. to develop their libraries and library collections. The institutions receiving grants or assistance in other forms mainly comprise universities including agricultural universities, research institutions, and colleges. The grants came from a variety of sources: India Wheat Loan Educational Exchange Program, Indo-US Technical Cooperation Program, Ford Foundation, Rockefeller Foundation and Asia Foundation. The present chapter provides an account of how they were helped in their library development through the aid received from these sources.

2. INDIA WHEAT LOAN EDUCATIONAL EXCHANGE PROGRAM

Foremost among the sources which assisted Indian universities and research institutions to develop their libraries and library collections was the India Wheat Loan Educational Exchange Program (IWLEEP). This was the "largest and most complex U.S. aid program involving a single country's [i. e. India's] university development during 1950s".[1]

The origin of the IWLEEP goes back to 1951, when the U.S. Congress granted a loan of $190 million (Rs. 98. 48 crores) to India for purchase of two million tons of foodgrains from the U.S. to meet the food crisis resulting from floods and drought in 1950. The loan was granted under the "India Emergency Food Act" (Public Law 48, 82nd

Congress, 1st session) wherein the provision was also made that the first $ 5 million paid by India as interest on loan was to be placed in a special deposit account in the Treasury of the U.S. for the rehabilitation and/or development of the Indian universities and institutions of higher learning. It was also agreed that the programme might be spread over five years and approximately $ 1,000,000 spent every year.[2]

The programme, which started functioning from 1954-55, helped Indian Universities in four specific ways:

(i) by assisting in the development of their library collections;
(ii) by providing an opportunity to thirty-five librarians to visit the U.S. to observe the working of major libraries there;
(iii) by organizing library workshops for the librarians who were sent to the U.S. ; and
(iv) by establishing extension libraries at Ludhiana, Madurai and Udaipur.

All these aspects of the programme are discussed below.

2.1 Assistance in the Development of Library Collections

Public Law 48 provided that "American scientific, technical and other scholarly works as well as books of American literature may be supplied to Indian institutions".[3] The medium of instruction in the Indian universities being English, universities and institutions of higher learning needed books and back files of periodicals in English to make their educational programmes more fruitful. They had to look towards the U. K. and U. S. for mitigating the book famine prevailing in the country. In these circumstances, the Wheat Loan book programme was a god-send for them.[4] An unique opportunity on an unprecedented scale was opened up for a free flow of much-needed American books and periodicals.[5]

The allocation of approximately $ 1,400,000 was made to a total of ninety-one institutions which included thirty-six universities, fifty-two research libraries and three university extension libraries. It was determined largely by the University Grants Commission which was, at the same time, making grants for book purchases from its own funds.[6] Table 3.1, which shows the distribution of book grants to various universities and research institutions, reveals that the grants varied from less than $ 500 to as much as $ 77,000 which indicates that the administrators of the Wheat Loan programme wanted to assist as many institutions as possible. Taking into consideration the budgetary provisions made for library purchases in Indian institutions during those days, it can be said that even the "smallest" amount (less than $ 500) was, after all, not that small.

TABLE 3.1: Distribution of Book Grants to Vavious Institutions in India under the India Wheat Loan Educational Exchange Program

Number of institutions	Allotment to each institution
Universities	
5	Between $ 65,000 and $77,000
8	Between $ 25,000 and $36,000
13	Between $ 15,000 and $24,500
10	Between $ 3,000 and $13,000
36	
Non-university research libraries	
1	$ 47,800
3	Between $ 16,000 and $28,000
8	Between $ 5,000 and $10,000
7	Between $ 2,500 and $3,500
22	Between $ 600 and $2,275
11	$ 500 or less
52	
University extension libraries	
3	$ 75,000[7]

Public Law 48 specified that the Wheat Loan funds must be used to purchase only American books, and, as such, all the institutions were required to confine their selection to American books so far as utilisation of these funds was concerned. Even for selecting titles, many institutions lacked the necessary bibliographical tools. The Wheat Loan Office in India, therefore, requested multiple copies of standard bibliographical tools and also sought selected lists of titles prepared by specialists in many subject fields. The bibliographical tools included time-honoured titles such as *Cumulative Book Index*, Winchell's *Guide to Reference Books*, *Ulrich's International Periodicals Directory*, *Books in Print* etc. These tools helped Indian librarians not only in selecting and acquiring books but also in preparing reading lists and compiling bibliographies useful to their readers.

A wide variation, reflecting the needs of individual libraries, can be observed in the types of publications added to the collections of the recipient institutions under the Wheat Loan Program. Numerous textbooks in many fields were acquired, but they did not make up a large percentage of the total purchases. The largest group of books acquired might be characterized as standard works in various fields which were in print at the time of ordering. A considerable number of librarians took advantage of this grant to purchase reference works such as bibliographies, printed catalogues, encyclopedias, yearbooks, dictionaries, etc. During the past two years of the Program, there was a shift in emphasis toward the purchase of back files of journals; so also, in a few instances, these grants were used for non-book materials, most often for back files of journals on micro-film and micro-fiche. In order to encourage such purchases and facilitate their use, permission was granted to libraries to buy microfilm and micro-fiche readers with the Wheat Loan funds.[8] The role of the Wheat Loan Book Program in strengthening Indian University libraries cannot be overstated.

2.2 Indian Librarians Visiting the U.S.

Public Law 48 also provided that its funds might be used to enable Indian professors, research workers and *other academic persons* to go to the U.S. for observation, studies, instruction, technical training or other educational activities. Accordingly, during the years 1955-60, the programme sponsored study tour of thirty-five Indian librarians from universities and research institutions to the U.S. "to absorb new ideas and library techniques and learn of bibliographical services which they could apply to their own particular library problems".[9]

These librarians were sent in four different batches as shown in Table 3.2. Most of them were working in universities; however, a few others working in research institutions were also included in the teams, as shown in Table 3.3. They were at different hierarchical levels such as librarians, deputy librarians, assistant librarians, etc., which is seen from Table 3.4. Thus, the selection of librarians was made with the twin objects of giving representation to a wide variety of libraries and providing opportunity to different categories of personnel to visit the U.S.

The grantees, on their return, submitted reports to their respective institutions; a few of them such as, for example, Das Gupta, Banerjea and Khandwala published their reports describing what they found noteworthy in American libraries and preffered suggestions for the development of libraries at home.[10-12]

TABLE 3.2: Number of Indian librarians (batchwise) sent to the U.S. under the Wheat Loan Program

Batch No	Year	Number of participants
1	1955	12
2	1956	11
3	1959	4
4	1960	5
	Total:	32 *

* Their names are given in Appendix VIII.
Note : Information regarding the other three participants could not be traced.

TABLE 3.3: Number of Indian librarians (Institutionwise) sent to the U.S. under the Wheat Loan Program

	Kind of institution	First batch	Second batch	Third batch.	Fourth batch	Total
1.	Universities	7	8	4	5	24
2.	Scientific libraries	2	—	—	—	2
3.	Polytechnics	1	—	—	—	1
4.	Indian Institutes of Technology	—	1	—	—	1
5.	Special libraries	1	1	—	—	2
6.	Engineering colleges	1	—	—	—	1
7.	National library	—	1	—	—	1
	Total:	12	11	4	5	32

TABLE 3.4: Number of Indian Library Professionals (Positionwise) sent to the U.S. under the Wheat Loan Program

	Position	First batch	Second batch	Third batch	Fourth batch	Total
1.	Librarians	9	5	1	3	18
2.	Deputy librarians	1	—	—	—	1
3.	Assistant librarians	2	5	3	2	12
4.	Others (Superintendent, Cataloguing division)	—	1	—	—	1
	Total:	12	11	4	5	32

The results of these visits had been most encouraging and may be grouped under four categories:

(i) personal development of the individual librarians concerned;
(ii) benefits that accrued to the institutions sponsoring the individuals;
(iii) general impact of the visits on the library movement in the country; and
(iv) better understanding between the two peoples.[13]

So far as the first two categories are concerned, the program yielded many benefits. It widened the outlook of the grantees and brought about a fresh orientation in their concept regarding books and libraries. It enriched their practical experience and enabled them to witness demonstrations of projects like the Farmington Plan, the Regional Bibliographical Centers, the National Union Catalog and the printing of the Library of Congress cards. It inspired them to emulate ideas like putting out attractive library guides, organizing orientation courses and book broadcasts, preparing staff manuals etc.[14] They appear to have acquired a heightened sense of mission. They were made aware of their legitimate status *vis-a-vis* the faculty and of the great educational role open to them.[15] The programme also enabled them to establish rapport with their counterparts. A bridge of friendship and a professional camaraderie developed out of this venture.[16] The value of this achievement in the realm of international understanding is inestimable.

2.3 Library Workshops

The second phase of the Wheat Loan Program was concerned with five library workshops–four on a zonal and one on a national basis–held in collaboration with the University Grants Commission and the Ministry of Education, Government of India, with the assumption that "a workshop exploits the dynamism of a group and the strength and complexity of interpersonal relationship in the group".[17] These workshops, which "were in the nature of a *grande finale* to the library project covering the years 1955-1961, were held at the following places on dates shown against them:

Baroda	December 18-23, 1960
Hyderabad	February 4-11, 1961
Patna	March 11-16, 1961

Jaipur	April 22-29, 1961
Delhi	March 5-9, 1962.[18]

The first four workshops were organized by Beatrice Holt and directed by Laurence J. Kipp who was assisted by Cecilia Rae Kipp. These workshops served as a follow-up device for evaluating the programme, provided added professional stimulation to the grantees and also gave them an opportunity to deliberate collectively to solve common problems.[19]

The first workshop, held at Baroda, was attended by fifteen librarians from the Western part of India. They were either grantees who had visited the U.S. under the Wheat Loan Program or were those who merely belonged to libraries which were recipients of the Wheat Loan book grants. Osmania University at Hyderabad played host to the second workshop, which was attended by seventeen participants from the South zone. The Patna workshop, third in the series, covered the Eastern zone of the country and was attended by seventeen participants. The fourth and the last zonal workshop for Northern zone was hosted by the University of Rajasthan (Jaipur) and was attended by ten librarians, including the five who had recently returned from a study and observation tour of the libraries in the U.S. and four members of the Action Committees of the former three workshops.[20]

The fifth and final workshop, held at Delhi, was arranged "to take stock of what had been achieved during the preceding period and to establish a permanent corporate body in order to continue the work begun at the workshops".[21] This follow-up workshop was also aimed at creating in high circles a favourable climate for the implementation of the decisions taken at the earlier workshops. The results achieved fulfilled the expectations, since prominent educationists and representatives of the Governments of India and the U.S. associated themselves with its proceedings.[22] In this workshop, the constitution of the Indian Academic Libraries Association was approved; in addition, a permanent body of librarians, called the Indian Council for Library Development, was formed, which was to work for the development of libraries and librarianship in India.

Some of the results of these workshops were immediate. Several librarians returned home and immediately held staff meetings in order to inform their staff members and involve them in the decision-making process; nearly all of them compiled lists of their American holdings to send to the Wheat Loan Office for cumulation.[23]

Among the many decisions taken at these workshops, two which deserve special mention relate to compiling a Union List of American serials available in India, and establishing Indian Academic Libraries Association.

The Union List of American serials, which was published in 1966, lists 2,584 items.[24] As a reference tool, the list has proved of immense help to Indian librarians. However, in the absence of any agency to take care of it, it has never been updated.

Regarding the decision taken at the Jaipur workshop to establish the Indian Academic Libraries Association, some tentative steps were taken in 1963 which, however, proved infructuous. It was also planned to bring out a newsletter of the Association entitled *Library Messenger*. Its first and the only issue was published in October 1963.

The participants of the workshops had launched another newsletter, entitled *Wheat Loan Messenger*, with the sole purpose of keeping the recipients of the Wheat Loan study tour grants informed about what was being done by them that could be construed as a direct result of their American sojourn. Only two issues of the newsletter–the inaugural number for June 1961 in mimeographed form and the second number for December 1961 in printed from–were published.

The effects of these workshops upon the participants cannot be fully measured; however, the benefit they derived might best be summarised with this comment from one of them: "I feel that I was able to learn more about libraries and librarians in this country in one week than I would have done in a whole year. Separated as we librarians in this country are, our problems do not seem to us to be anybody else's concern. But, by this pooling of experiences and opinions without any reserve, we saw our problems now as patterns and the whole community of librarians engaged in coping with them."[25]

2.4 University Extension Libraries

The concept of extension library was quite novel when they were established in India. Lal provides a brief historical account of this idea and experiment.[26] Teachers and students of colleges affiliated to universities could not avail of university library facilities due to long distances. To remove this disparity in facilities, the planners at the University Grants Commission conceived the idea of extension library.[27] The Wheat Loan Program provided substantial grants for the establishment of three extension libraries–one each at Madurai under the University of Madras, at Ludhiana under the University of Panjab and at Udaipur under the University of Rajasthan.

2.4.1 Extension Library at Madurai: The extension library at Madurai was established in 1957, exactly one hundred years after the establishment of the University of Madras. Gnanamuttu and Chandran provide information on this library, the former by pointing out the effect of the Wheat Loan Program on the library and the latter by giving an account of its progress during the ten years.[28-29] Chandran also submitted a project report making an assessment of the development of the library.[30]

The library started with a modest collection of 1,500 books in 1957. Between 1957 and 1960, the Wheat Loan Program gave a sum of $ 75,000 that was utilised for purchase of books and periodicals of American origin which formed what came to be called the "Lincoln Collection". In addition, the United States Information Service and the Asia Foundation donated a large quantity of books and rare materials. The library also received a good number of books from the Book of the Month Club of the U.S. The result was that by 1966, the library had acquired nearly 30,000 volumes.

A rather unusual aspect worth mentioning about the library is that whereas most university libraries get established after the establishment of the university itself, here was a library which was started long before the departments were established by the University of Madras at Madurai. This was a case where the University took a cue from the Radhakrishnan Commission (1948-49) that the library is the heart of all academic activity of the University.[31] The University of Madras could not have succeeded in this effort but for the assistance it received from the Wheat Loan Program, the USIS and the Asia Foundation.

2.4.2 Extension Libraries at Ludhiana and Udaipur: Established in 1960, the Extension Library at Ludhiana received the sums of $ 50,000 for books and $ 25,000 for furnitures under the Wheat Loan Program during the same year. During the next three years, it acquired books from this grant and also received donations of books from the Asia Foundation, American Embassy (Delhi) and U.S. Book Exchange. Table 3.5 which summarizes these purchases and donations, makes it clear that during a short span of four years, 16,587 books and 497 serials were added to the library through different U.S. sources.

TABLE 3.5: Number of Monographs/Serials added to the Extension Library, Ludhiana during 1961-1964

Source	1961	1962	1963	1964	Total
1. Purchase under the Wheat Loan Program	3,905	8,435	142	—	12,482
2. Gift from Asia Foundation, U.S.A.	1,308 170(S)	—	—	—	1,308 170(S)
3. Gift from American Embassy, New Delhi	760	144	—	—	904
4. Gift from U.S. Book Exchange, Washington (D.C.)	—	61 327(S)	—	130	191 327(S)
5. Gift from Asia Foundation, Delhi	—	—	—	1,702	1,702
Total	5,973 170 (S)	8,640 327(S)	142 —	1,832 —	16,587 497(S)

Note: (S) - Serials.

The Extension Library at Udaipur also received a sum of $ 75,000 for purchase of American books. In due course of time, the Extension libraries at Madurai and Udaipur were upgraded into university libraries for the new universities established at those places. The one at Ludhiana remains the only Extension library.

In evaluating these Extension libraries, Lal believes that "such a project can be very useful in developing countries like India".[32] In this context, Kipps' observations and expectations are worth mentioning. "These new libraries", they observe, "are to serve affiliated colleges in centers some distance from the universities. They are to offer collections and services which will supplement inadequate libraries in the colleges. . . . In order to succeed, they must reach out to interest faculty and students of the colleges, offer attractive open-shelf collections and develop the best of reference services. . . . If these libraries succeed, they will provide excellent demonstration not only to nearby colleges but to other communities where it would be appropriate to establish libraries for joint use of the colleges. This is experimental librarianship but. . . we think that the concept may be of real value to India. Hence, this use of Wheat Loan funds is most appropriate".[33] Indeed, it was. Not only two extension libraries were upgraded as university libraries, but some other universities in the country also established extension libraries at their post-graduate centres which later developed into universities. Gulbarga, Warangal (Kakatiya) and Anantpur (Sri Krishna Devaraya) are cases in point.

2.5 IWLEEP: An Evaluation

Considered as a whole, the Wheat Loan Program gave a great impetus to university libraries in the country by making available the much-needed book grants. A select number of university librarians professionally benefited by the tour of the U.S. which enabled them to enhance their practical experience. This helped them to raise their standard to the level equal to the demands of emerging scholarship in free India.[34] In addition, the exchange of visits has established a permanent liaison between American and Indian librarianship.[35] According to Inamdar and Riswadkar, the impact of the Wheat Loan Program was three-fold: librarianship in India was more directly exposed to the state of the art in the U.S.; Indian academic librarians realized the importance of reader services and they also recognized that they themselves could find solutions to ever-present problems.[36]

The impact of the aid received under the programme is manifest not only in the enriched collections of books and journals in Indian university libraries, but it is also apparent in the change in approach and outlook of Indian librarians towards the profession. "It is no exaggeration to assert that but for this god-send, development of Indian university libraries would have been retarded and remained backward".[37] The Wheat Loan Program has had a percolating effect since the full impact of it was felt not only by the generation of Indian librarians who participated in its manifold aspects, but also by others of the succeeding generations.

3. INDO-AMERICAN TECHNICAL CO-OPERATION PROGRAM

Another U.S. Government-sponsored programme, though not as wide in its coverage as the Wheat Loan Program was the Indo American Technical Co-operation Program. Its essential purpose was "to make available knowledge, techniques, men and material of the U.S. for the economic and social development of India".[38] The Program dates from the signing of the general agreement between the Governments of India and the U.S. on 5 January, 1952. Since then the two countries have signed numerous agreements covering a large number of projects in support of India's Five-Year Plans. Though no particular agreement was signed in support of any project concerning library field *per se*, parts of the sums provided to various institutions under different agreements were utilized for library collection development. For example, out of the amount of $1,034,461 provided for the village workers training programme under agreement No. 7, sums were made available for the acquisition from outside India of books, audio-visual instructional and demonstrational supplies and equipment for the training centres, and for financing motion-pictures and film-strips to be locally produced. Under Agreement No. 15, some part of U.S. funds of $ 100,000 was used by the Central Labour Institute at Bombay for purchase of technical books. Under Agreement No. 27, library materials were provided to the Public Administration Centre at Lucknow University. Under another agreement, the U.S. provided a set of approximately 400 books and periodicals on management for the particular use of the industry and management research unit of the Indian Statistical Institute at Calcutta.[39]

Among all the agreements signed between the two governments under the above programme, Agreement No. 41 concerning home science education and research in India deserves special mention. At the time when the Technical Co-operation Program was in operation, the study of home science or home economics was relatively new in India. However, its importance in raising living standards had already been recognized and education and research in it was developing rapidly in Indian institutions of higher learning.

On 31 May, 1955, an agreement under the Technical Co-operation Program was executed between the two Governments for the purpose of providing to selected Indian colleges and universities technical assistance, training opportunities, equipment and supplies with a view to assisting in the programme of developing and strengthening home science education and research in India. Colleges and universities were chosen for assistance under this programme on the recommendations of the Home Science Association of India.[40]

Under the Agreement, which was operative for three years in the first instance from 1 June, 1955, provision was made for $ 100,000 worth of books and equipment.[41] The scope and coverage of the project was extended for another three years under Supplement I to Operational Agreement 41 on 29 April, 1958. Under this supplement, assistance was to be provided on a regional, rather than institutional, basis and was to be channelled through demonstrational centres located at (a) Lady Irwin College, New Delhi (North India), (b) Viharilal Mitra

Institute, Calcutta (East India), (c) S. N. D. T. Women's University, Bombay (West India), and (d) S. I. E. T. College for Women, Madras (South India). The Supplement provided for the assistance worth $ 80,000 for books and equipment.[42] The amounts granted for purchase of books were way beyond what the recipient institutions could ever have obtained from any other source for their collection development. Thus, though the Indo-American Technical Cooperation Program did not directly cover the field of librarianship, it enormously helped many institutions in different subject fields to develop their library collections.

4. CONTRIBUTION OF PHILANTHROPIC ORGANIZATIONS TO LIBRARY COLLECTION DEVELOPMENT IN INDIA

Along with the Government-sponsored programmes discussed above, non-governmental organizations, especially foundations, have generously supported overseas library assistance projects. Of the four foundations which have played an important role in the field of librarianship at the international level, two, viz. the Ford Foundation and the Rockefeller Foundation, have had closest relationship with the ALA's International Relations Office in such endeavours. Their annual reports reveal a major commitment to large-scale programmes of international development. The other two foundations, viz., the Carnegie Corporation and the Asia Foundation, have been involved in international library advisory activities, but to a much lesser extent than the former two.[43]

4.1 Carnegie Corporation

Although the Carnegie Corporation is the oldest of the four foundations and has the longest history of overseas library aid in one form or another[44], it "has not provided funding for libraries in India and it has never had a grant program of any type in India".[45] Why the Corporation did not regard India as deserving of its munificence is difficult to surmise, but with the exception of Hong Kong and Malaysia, no other Asian country was fortunate enough to be a beneficiary of its world-wide library programme.

4.2 Rockefeller Foundation

The Rockefeller Foundation was founded in 1913 with a substantial endowment and a charter pledging it to the "well-being of mankind". At first, the Foundation concentrated on man's basic needs; in the early years, that meant control of disease, then establishment of public health services, and later, training of medical personnel. Grants in the social sciences began in 1928 and the agricultural program was begun in 1940.[46]

The Foundation's activities in India started with the establishment of public health services and date back to 1916, when public health workers of the International health Commission collaborated in surveys of the incidence of hookworm in the country. The Foundation also maintained one or more resident representatives in India.

The Foundation's annual reports for the past few years reveal that, in India, it began to provide grants for one or the other purpose relevant to library field since 1954. During the subsequent thirteen years, grants were provided for various library purposes such as purchase of books, construction or extension of library buildings, recruitment of library staff, library training and visits of librarians to other countries for library work.

So far as the library and information science field is concerned, twenty institutions and four individuals in India were provided with grants. The institutions include six universities, five academic and research institutions in agriculture, four academic and research institutions in medicine, a home science college, a state government and three other institutions. Individual librarians working in different types of libraries were provided with grants either to visit libraries in other countries, to consult library specialists, or to collect library material from foreign countries for their own libraries.

4.2.1 Grants to Universities: The six universities which received grants were Karnatak University, Dharwad; Patna University, Patna; M. S. University of Baroda, Baroda; Andhra University, Waltair; Agra University, Agra; and University of Delhi, Delhi.

The Karnatak University and Agra University were provided with grants of $ 1,000 and $ 2,050 respectively to purchase books, the former for books on language, literature and culture and the latter for books for the library of its Institute of Social Sciences. The other three universities, viz. those at Baroda, Patna and Waltair, were provided with about $ 1,100 each to conduct surveys of conditions and prospects for university publishing in India.

The University of Delhi received grants for three of its

departments–those of Comparative Music Studies, Economics and Commerce, and Library Science. In 1958, it received $ 106,850 for establishing and developing the new institute of music. The grant, which was to be utilized through the period ending 30 June, 1964, was used among other things, for recruiting library staff, acquiring essential books, musical scores, records and other equipments. In 1966, the Department of Economics and Commerce received $ 6,750 for equipment and library. The third grant related to library science education.

4.2.2 Grants to Academic and Research Institutions in Agriculture: Five academic and research institutions in agriculture and one state government received large grants, part or whole of which was spent by them in procuring books for their libraries and for extending their library buildings. The institutions include Punjab Agricultural University, Ludhiana; Horticultural Research Station of the Government of Uttar Pradesh; Central Rice Research Institute, Cuttack; Indian Agricultural Research Institute, New Delhi; Balwant Rajput College, Agra; and Ministry of Agriculture, West Bengal.

In 1963, the Punjab Agricultural University at Ludhiana received $ 320,000 to be spent over a period of five years, a part of which was utilized to procure books and periodicals. The Horticultural Research Station of the Government of Uttar Pradesh reveived a two-year grant of $ 47,000 in 1955 and the Central Rice Research Institute at Cuttack received a grant of $ 125,000 in 1958 for a three-year period. In both these cases, a part of the grant was utilized for purchase of library materials.

The Indian Agricultural Research Institute at Delhi received grants twice–first in 1958 and subsequently in 1961. The grant provided in 1958 was utilized for the construction of a new wing to the library building since the stacks in the building then existing were already utilized to full capacity. The Foundation appropriated $ 100,000 to defray the costs of the new wing for the library, which was to furnish additional space for the growing collection of books and periodicals, for reading rooms and for microfilming and photostat services. The subsequent grant of $ 45,000, made during 1961 through October 1964, was utilized to purchase equipment for the library.

Balwant Rajput College at Bichpuri, Agra, an affiliate of the University of Agra, is one of India's principal centres for agricultural teaching and research, which has long been interested in meeting the educational needs of India's rural population and has been particularly successful in bridging the gap between agricultural theory and local practice. To help meet the costs of equipment and library facilities at the Bichpuri centre, the Foundation appropriated $ 200,000 in 1958 to the college. Similarly, in 1959, a grant of $ 65,000 was made to the Ministry of Agriculture, West Bengal, for acquiring library books needed at a rural university proposed for the state in lieu of the research facilities lost to East Pakistan (now Bangladesh).

4.2.3 Grants to Academic and Research Institutions in Medicine: In the field of medicine, Christian Medical College at Vellore, King George's Medical College of the University of Lucknow, the Institute of Child Health, Calcutta, and the National Institute of Virology Pune, were beneficiaries of grants from the Foundation.

4.2.3.1 Christian Medical College, Vellore: In order to enable the Christian Medical College at Vellore to establish a Hospital Record System, the Foundation gave it a grant of Rs. 39,300 (about $ 8,650) in 1954. Later, two more grants of Rs. 14,500 (about $ 3,160) and $ 21,000 for a two-year period were made in 1957 and in 1958 with the expectation that the well-run medical record library department of the College would serve as a demonstration and guide for other Indian medical institutions.

4.2.3.2 King George's Medical College, Lucknow: King George's Medical College of the University of Lucknow, which has one of the best medical libraries in India, had, sometime in 1958, plans to enlarge its library collection, open a rental library, add to its audio-visual equipment and establish a documentation unit. The new documentation unit was to enable the library to provide reference services for other institutions in India, while the expansion of the audio-visual unit was to permit the college staff to display medical and paramedical films as a regular feature of the teaching programme. A grant of $ 34,000 was given in 1958 to the University to assist the continued development of the central library's services at King George's Medical College during the period ending June 30, 1961. The grant was chiefly to be used for buying equipment and for reconversion of the library building to provide the additional space needed for the new units.

A possibility of including a selected number of standard textbooks to a rental library of the college was suggested to the college authorities by the foundation office at Delhi. The college accepted the suggestion and rental library became operative. Provision in the college library for non-book materials like audio-visual aids, microfilming documents, reference and abstract services, as well as scientific documentation was also made. The audio-visual aids unit started functioning in 1965. The unit has more than justified itself by producing scientific documentation aids and by making communication of scientific knowledge easier.

4.2.3.3 National Institute of Virology, Pune: The Virus Research Centre at Pune, renamed as the National Institute of Virology in August 1978, was established in 1952 by the Indian Council of Medical Research, with assistance from the Foundation and the Government of Bombay. it was maintained jointly by the Indian Council of Medical Research and the Foundation up to the year 1967. The annual reports of the centre for the years 1958-71 show that during these years, the centre utilized part of the Foundation grant for purchase of books for its library and developed a collection of 3,703 volumes by 1971. The centre ceased to receive any grant from the Foundation from 1972 onwards.

4.2.3.4 Institute of Child Health, Calcutta: The Institute of Child Health at Calcutta was established in 1953 as a private organization for teaching and research in pediatrics. It has been approved and encouraged by the State and Central Governments and is affiliated to the University of Calcutta, which in 1957, recognized it as a post-graduate centre. In order to enable the Institute to have a modern teaching and research programme embracing the major types of pediatric activity, the Foundation appropriated $ 45,000 to it in 1958 as a three-year grant. This was to be utilized, among other things, for the development of the library. Between 1958 and 1960, the Institute was able to add to its library collection about 1,200 books through the grants. Out of the total collection of 4,800 volumes which required three decades to develop, 25 per cent was added during a span of three years with the Foundation assistance !

4.2.4 Grants to other Institutions: Along with the aforesaid institutions, imparting instructions or carrying out research in one faculty or another, four more institutions, three from Delhi and one from Coimbatore, were provided with substantial grants by the Foundation for their library development. These institutions were the Indian School of International Studies, Delhi; the Asian-African Consultative Committee, Delhi; Sri Avinashilingam Home Science College, Coimbatore, and the India International Centre, Delhi. So also, one more institution, viz. the Indian Council of World Affairs, Delhi, was provided the grant, not for the library development, but for the study of Indo-American relations.

4.2.4.1 Indian School of International Studies, Delhi: Soon after India's attainment of independence, a group of the country's leading citizens and scholars began planning the organization of a school to offer advanced training in basic social science disciplines, in international affairs, and in the history and institutions of countries or regions of particular importance to India's foreign affairs. These efforts resulted in the establishment in 1955 of the Indian School of International Studies in Delhi as a national centre for doctoral study and advanced research in the field. In 1957, the Foundation provided the school with a grant or $ 50,000 and again in 1962 with another grant of $ 150,000 for its library development. The funds provided in 1957 were to be utilized for the purchase of important library materials during the next seven years; those provided in 1962 were intended principally for developing its collections of research materials on the major areas of Asia. The East-Asian Research Center of Harvard University, directed by John K. Fairbank, cooperated in the selection and acquisition of the new collection.

The Asian-African Consultative Committee, which had its permanent Secretariat in New Delhi, was provided with grants by the Foundation twice–$ 2,500 in 1958 and $ 350 in the following year for purchase of publications in international law and related fields. So also, Sri Avinashilingam Home Science College at Coimbatore, which specialized in home science education, received a grant of $ 5,000 in 1961 for purchase of textbooks and other library material; whereas the India International Centre at Delhi received from the Foundation operational grants in the first few years of its activities which included the running of a library. Over the years, the Centre's library has grown gradually and has at present a collection of more than 20,000 volumes.

4.2.4.2 Indian Council of World Affairs, Delhi: The Foundation's grant in 1954 to the Indian Council of World Affairs, Delhi deserves special mention, though it was not related to the library development of the Council. In an effort to promote mutual understanding between India and the U.S., the Council undertook in 1954 a study of Indo-American relations, in cooperation with the Council on Foreign Relations, New York. To cover the cost of the Indian Council's participation in this project, the Foundation appropriated in 1954 an amount of $ 20,050 which was to be available for a two-year period. The grant, though not directly related to library field, is mentioned here in appreciation of the Foundation's role in promoting mutual understanding between the U.S. and India.[47]

4.2.5 Grants to Individual Librarians: The Foundation also provided grants to four individual librarians either to visit libraries in the U.S. for observation or to collect materials from the U.S. for their libraries. With the financial assistance of $ 5,050 in 1959 and a supplementary grant of $ 250 in 1960, Kapil Deo Singh, Librarian of Balwant Rajput College at Bichpuri, Agra, was able to visit centres of library science in U.S. and Canada. Girja Kumar, Librarian of the Indian Council of World Affairs at New Delhi, was provided with a grant of $ 3,850 in 1962 to visit major social science research libraries, and to consult classification specialists in Europe and the U.S. concerning his research on library classification in the social sciences with particular reference to international relations. A grant of $ 2,380 in 1965 enabled S. P. Phadnis of the Indian Agricultural Research Institute, New Delhi to visit libraries in Europe and the U.S. to collect materials from there for the Institute's library; and Dr. Subhadra Chitale, a qualified doctor and a librarian in the Directorate General of Health Services, Government of India, New Delhi, was given a grant of $ 3,300 in 1966 to visit the U.S. National Library of Medicine and library centres in Chicago and Rome.

4.2.6 Evaluation: In evaluating the Foundation's role, it can appropriately be said that these grants to various institutions in India for their library development bear out Fosdick's remarks that the contribution of the Foundation to the intellectual life of the world and the well-being of mankind can scarcely be questioned.[48] The Foundation has doubtless earned the gratitude and respect of many people in many lands including, of course, India.

4.3 Ford Foundation

The Ford Foundation was established in 1936 under Michigan Laws by

Henry Ford and members of his family as a vehicle for some of their charitable concerns. From its earliest days, the Foundation gave top priority to education and research and this is apparent from the Foundation's support in improving schools at all levels, technical and vocational education, educational leadership, advancement and strengthening of higher education.[49] The Foundation has contributed considerable amounts to library fields in its domestic and international operations. In the case of developing countries too, a number of major grants have been made exclusively for library development there; also many grants which were made primarily for other purposes, contained peripheral support for library development.

So far as the Foundation's contribution to India is concerned, it can be seen that from the beginning of India's First Five-Year Plan in 1951, it has helped the nation explore new approaches to age-old problems and find new ways of developing its economy and society. Its aid to India is directed towards helping her basic development activities calculated to strengthen the economic and social welfare of her people.[50] The Foundation itself has brought out two publications providing information about its activities in India.[51-52] The first provides description of various activities supported by it, and the latter presents a summary of its grants from 1951 to 1969 to support these activities. The Foundation supported activities in varied subject fields such as agriculture and rural development, industrial and business development, education and public administration.

So far as the Foundation's grants to library development in India are concerned, institutions working in the fields mentioned above received both types of grants viz. grants made exclusively for library development and peripheral support for library development included in grants made primarily for other purposes. During 1951-69, twelve institutions in different fields received grants related to library development. The information about these institutions and the years in which they received grants from the Foundation is provided in Table 3.6. Except the University of Delhi, all the remaining institutions received grants for other purposes, and part of these was utilized by the concerned institutions for library development.

4.3.1 Grants to University of Delhi: As many as five departments/faculties in the University of Delhi were provided with grants by the Foundation and a part of these grants was utilized by them for library collection development. The departments/faculties

TABLE 3.6. Names of Institutions and the years in which they received from the Ford Foundation during the years 1954-70

Sr. No.	Name of the Institution	1954	1955	1956	1957	1958	1959	1960	1961	1962	1963	1964	1965	1966	1967	1968	1969	1970	$	Amount
1.	National Design Institute, Delhi								*	*	*								$	1,100,000
2.	Shri Ram Centre for Industrial Relations, Delhi											*			*				$	325,000
3.	Banaras Hindu University, Varanasi											*			*				$	544,000
4.	University of Delhi, Delhi																			
	Chinese Studies												--- Six-year period ---						$	536,000
	Department of Linguistics												* Four-year period						$	200,000
	Law Faculty														* Two years				$	441,000
	Library Development														* Three years				$	351,000
	American History and Civilization		*			*	*												$	238,000
5.	Birla Institute of Technology and Science, Pilani		*									*	Seven-year period		*				$	1629,446
	Massachusetts Institute of Technology												* Seven-year period						$	1,450,000
6.	Indian Institute of Public Administration, New Delhi	*								*				*		*			$	1,189,500
7.	Administrative Staff College of India, Hyderabad					*						*							$	931,143
8.	National Academy of Administration, New Delhi								*										$	62,500
9.	Institute of Constitutional and Parliamentary Studies, New Delhi														* Three years				$	200,000
10.	Literacy House, Lucknow				*														$	69,000
11.	Southern Languages Book Trust, Madras		*				*					*							$	599,500
12.	Indian Law Institute, New Delhi				*	*			*										$	622,500

* Indicates the year in which the grant was received.

included Department of Chinese Studies, Department of Linguistics, Department of American History, Library Department and the Law faculty. The University of Delhi was the only institution in India which received, in addition to a number of grants from the Foundation, one exclusively for library development, credit for which goes to Dr. C. D. Deshmukh, the then Vice-Chancellor of the University. To quote him:

> The coping-stone of my tenure [as the Vice-Chancellor of the University of Delhi] was. . . the financial support I was able to enlist for the development of the University during the Fourth and Fifth Five-Year Plan periods. Dr. Douglas Ensminger of the Ford Foundation had. . . been anxious to help a couple of universities in India to raise their standards and status to the level attained by leading universities of the world. At one time he and I (as the Chairman of the University Grants Commission) thought that assistance for this purpose would be most effective if used for helping build up a new university *ab initio*. However, after gaining some experience of and insight into the situation of Delhi University I formed the view that the University had a high potential and the contemplated help if given to it would yield maximum return in the shortest possible period. I shared this conclusion with Dr. Ensminger and was glad to find him in agreement. . . . Although the bulk of the assistance was earmarked for the science faculty and its costly equipment, central services, chiefly the Library, received their due share.[53]

The Foundation's grant of $ 1. 1 million was utilized by the University from 1968 to 1979 in developing the library facilities by acquiring the latest books and important research journals.[54]

4.3.2 Grants to other Institutions: A couple of other institutions which had received the Foundation grants do deserve special mention. The India Literacy Board received in 1957 a grant of $ 69,000 to assist the Literacy House in its programme for producing reading materials for new literates.[55] Taking into consideration the percentage of illiterates in India and the government efforts to remove illiteracy, the contribution made by the Foundation was as timely as precious. So also, the Southern Languages Book Trust, formed by the Vice-Chancellors of South Indian universities, received the Foundation support thrice, in 1955, 1959 and 1963, for its programme of publication, distribution and marketing of high-quality low-priced books in the four South Indian regional languages–Tamil, Telugu, Malayalam and Kannada. The total grant which the Trust received from the Foundation amounted to $ 599,500.[56]

4.3.2.1 G. B. Pant University of Agriculture and Technology, Pantnagar: G. B. Pant University of Agriculture and Technology at Pantnagar received a grant of $ 120,500 to support the establishment of India's first Agricultural Communication Centre there. Though not strictly for library development, the grant enabled the university to purchase a variety of modern audio-visual, press and radio recording equipment not available in India. The university library's stock was also augmented with the latest books and periodicals in the field of communication.[57]

4.3.3 Grants during 1970s and 1980s: Even during 1970s and 1980s, the Foundation continued to provide grants to various institutions in India, some of which at least have partially used them for their library development. The Foundation itself has neither published any *summary of grants* nor provided any details of the grants in its annual reports. Nevertheless, information that could be reliably gathered shows that eight institutions utilized the funds partially for their library development. These institutions include G. B. Pant Social Science Institute, Allahabad; Centre for Policy Research, Centre for the Study of Developing Societies, Institute of Economic Growth (University of Delhi) (all from Delhi); Indian School of Political Economy, Lonavala; Giri Institute of Development Studies, Lucknow; Deccan College Post-Graduate and Research Institute, Pune; and Indian Institute of Education, Pune.

4.3.3.1 G. B. Pant Social Science Institute, Allahabad: The Foundation provided to the Institute a grant of $ 100,000 in 1983 which was to be utilized during the next three years. Out of the total grant, the sum of $ 35,000 was earmarked for purchase of books and journals including back volumes, and $ 25,000 was to be utilized for purchasing reprographic and documentation facilities and other equipment for library development. So also, $ 30,000 was to be utilized for purchasing a computer with word processor and offset printer and modern cartographic equipment.[58]

4.3.3.2 Centre for Policy Research, New Delhi: The Centre received grants of $ 160,000 and $ 150,000 in 1980 and 1983. Out of these grants, $ 92,000 and $ 55,000 were utilized for improving the centre's library resources.[59]

4.3.3.3 Centre for the Study of Developing Societies, Delhi: The centre received grants twice–first in 1977 and again in 1984. Out of the first grant, $ 35,000 were spent on library support including storage and bibliographic services; from the second grant, an amount of Rs. 2.90 lakhs was allocated for overall library development.[60]

4.3.3.4 Institute of Economic Growth, University of Delhi, Delhi: The Institute's library, built over a period of about two decades, is considered to be one of the best economics libraries in India. However, because of the steep rise in book prices and journal subscription, the Institute found it difficult to maintain its current subscriptions, let alone taking out new ones. For the same reason, the Institute could hardly acquire more than a modicum of new publications in economics and related subjects of interest to it. Out of the total grant of $ 260,000, the Institute therefore utilized $ 60,000 for subscribing to new journals and acquiring back volumes of other journals to augment or complete their runs, and for adding new publications.[61]

4.3.3.5 Indian School of Political Economy, Lonavala: In April 1975, the Foundation sanctioned a grant of $ 125,000 to the School for development support. The main objective of the School is to conduct a series of short-term courses for public workers in various walks of life and produce and publish relevant literature, for which the Foundation, through this grant, has provided the necessary infrastructure. Out of the total grant of Rs. 10,80,221.48 ($ 125,000), an amount of Rs. 3,45,677.88 was spent by the School in strengthening its library collections.[62]

4.3.3.6 Giri Institute of Development Studies, Lucknow: The Foundation provided to the Institute a grant of $ 150,000 for the purpose of developing research and training facilities. The grant commenced during 1980-81 and was to be utilized during the next three years. The grant came to the Institute at its initial stage of development and helped it to a significant extent in that direction.

The most important respect in which the grant helped the Institute was in the building of its library as, out of the total grant, approximately Rs. 7 lakhs was spent on library development during 1980-83. During this period, about 5,000 books and complete back volumes of some journals were procured. The number of journals subscribed by the Institute rose from 83 in 1980 to 136 in 1983. The grant also facilitated purchase of necessary equipment for stacking and cataloguing books and journals. Another important item ancillary to library service, a photocopying machine, was also acquired from the grant funds.[63]

4.3.3.7 Deccan College Post-Graduate and Research Institute, Pune: In 1983, the College received a munificent grant of Rs. 21 lakhs, out of which Rs. 3 lakhs was earmarked by the College for purchase of books on archaeology. The grant was for three years and each year books worth Rs. 1 lakh ($ 10,000) were purchased for the library.[64]

4.3.3.8 Indian Institute of Education, Pune: In 1983, financial assistance of $ 200,000 was provided to the Institute for being utilized in the five-year period starting in October 1983. The Institute, reorganized by Dr. (Smt.) Chitra Naik and the late J. P. Naik in 1976, was growing rapidly in its activities, and its bourgeoning programme of teaching, training, extension and research called for improved library support. The high costs of books and journal subscriptions had virtually ruled out any significant expansion in library services, but the grant enabled the Institute to surmount that obstacle. The Institute set aside $ 50,000 for library development during the five-year span, spending substantially in the first year and tapering down in the subsequent years.[65]

4.4 Asia Foundation

A publicly supported non-profit philanthropic organization founded in 1954 and incorporated in the State of California, the Asia Foundation's major activity was in Asia where it had resident offices and programmes in twelve countries from Korea through Southeast Asia. The Foundation was interested in furthering civic, organizational and professional standards in Asia, and was concerned in part, therefore, with the state of library services in Asia. Consequently, its numerous activities specifically involved the development and improvement of library facilities in Asian countries.

In India, the Foundation confined its role primarily to developing library collections. Unlike other foundations such as the Rockefeller and Ford Foundations, the Asia Foundation did not provide grants but donated books through its 'Book for Asian Students Program', which was "one of the most imaginative programs of the Foundation".[66] Under this programme, the Foundation used to obtain books in the U.S. through gifts by American citizens and institutions, and bulk purchases of publishers' reminder .[67] These were then shipped to various institutions–universities, colleges and even secondary and elementary schools in various countries.

Realizing that the programme had a wider scope in India, the Foundation expanded its Book Program in this country. For this purpose it set up a warehouse in Delhi during the latter part of 1963. Books and journals started going out from the warehouse to Indian universities and colleges.[68]

The foundation shipped a total of 507,671 books and 171,401 journals to India. Most of these were sent during the period 1961-68 and were distributed by the New Delhi Office to educational institutions and other organizations throughout the country.[69] Though the exact number of institutions which received books from the Foundation is not known, it appears that by the end of April 1965, eighty-four institutions had received 90,055 books and 31,077 journals.[70] Among the beneficiary universities were those of Calcutta, Delhi, Bombay, Madras and Baroda;[71] however, details about colleges and secondary and elementary schools are not available.

Among other institutions which received books from the Foundation, the American Studies Research Centre at Hyderabad stands out. The centre has been receiving books under this programme since its establishment in 1964. From 1964 to June 1983, it received fifty-two shipments consisting of 34,389 books, 1010 volumes of bound periodicals and 13,042 issues of journals.[72] Carltan Lowenberg, former Director of Books for Asia Program, played a crucial role in assisting the centre in enriching its collection.[73] After his retirement in 1981, Richard Lamb took over the responsibility and continued to give the centre equally valuable service.

The significance of books programmes of the Asia Foundation can be brought out by saying that through them the Foundation increased the access of Asians to Western ideas and thoughts.

5. OTHER DONATIONS

Along with the Government-sponsored programmes and those of

philanthropic organizations described above, some other institutions and even individuals did present books, in small or large quantities, to institutions in India. Published records of all such donations are not available, and it is, unfortunately difficult to name all the benefactors or the beneficiaries. However, the following are some known instances.

5.1 Universal Serials and Book Exchange (Formerly United States Book Exchange)

The Universal Serials and Book Exchange (USBE), (formerly United States Book Exchange) is a self-supporting, non-governmental organization, which provides a clearing house for the co-operative exchange of duplicates and other publications between libraries throughout the world. Stocks of the USBE include items deposited by member libraries, primarily research serials from various countries, books from abroad and some out-of-print U.S. Publications. In the Indian context, it appears that many institutions, especially universities, availed themselves of this facility.

5.2 Donation of Books to Atomic Energy Commission, India

In 1955, the Atomic Energy Commission in India received a most valuable donation of 51,000 technical items for its library from the U.S. The donation included 6,525 technical reports, bound volumes of *National Nuclear Energy Series* and *Nuclear Science Abstracts* and 45,000 abstract cards which indexed and described all Atomic Energy Commission (U.S.) literature.[74]

5.3 Donation of Books to Supreme Court of India Library, New Delhi

Books on American law were presented to the Supreme Court of India Library by American lawyers who attended the International Congress of Jurists in New Delhi in January 1959 and who were much impressed by the judicial system in India. The gift was made as an expression of their gratitude for India's hospitality and friendship.[75]

5.4 Donation of Books by "Project India" Students of the University of California at Los Angeles (UCLA)

The "Project India" students of the University of California at Los Angeles (UCLA), who made a two-month goodwill tour of university centres throughout India, collected 30,000 American books in the U.S. and presented them to India. These books were distributed to select universities in India by the University Grants Commission.[76]

5.5 U.S. Children's Donation to India

A gift which could very well be the only of its kind is the U.S. children's donation of $ 25 to India in 1952. The amount was donated by children, making use of a village library in Ohio, to the Prime Minister's Relief Fund by saving sales tax stamps which were redeemable to buy extra books. The children decided to share the proceeds of the sales with other countries and out of the savings, donated $ 25 to India to be spent on children's books. In making this most unusual gift, the village Librarian remarked: "There are people in our village who take a very deep interest in India and who feel that what is going on there represents the finest political planning and moral thinking anywhere in the world today".[77] A tribute so touching and heart-warming is seldom received.

6. JOINT INDO-AMERICAN TEXTBOOK PROGRAM

Though the Joint Indo-American Textbook Program is furthest from being an undertaking for donation of books, it is included here as it made possible the reprinting in India of nearly two thousand American university and polytechnic textbooks, thus mitigating an almost endemic textbook famine. The Program, which was carried on in India during the decades of the 1960s and the 1970s, was established in India in response to a formal request of the Ministry of Education, Government of India. As per the Ministry's request, a body, designated as the joint Indo-American Textbook Board and made up of officials of the Ministry and the United States Information Agency (USIA), was constituted to set policies and to furnish administrative supervision for the Program.

Policies established by this board provided for review and approval of textbooks proposed by Indian publishers; for royalties to American publishers which were not to exceed 10 per cent of the U.S. list prices and subject to a 50 per cent Indian income-tax; for printing and binding of the reprint editions *in India*; and for sale to Indian students at one-fifth of the U.S. list prices.[78]

During the 1960s, rupee funds were made available for the Program under Public Law 480 of 83rd Congress. However, as the Program grew during the 1970s, this funding became inadequate to match the increasing requirements. The United States Agency for International

Development (USAID)'s Mission in India joined the Program in 1969 with $ 6 million in funding support in three instalments and became a co-sponsor of the Program, taking over funding for all scientific and technical books.[79]

In the first year of its operation, the Program sponsored the publication of only nineteen reprint editions of American textbooks with 49,000 copies. After several years of experience, and with greatly enhanced funding in the late 1960s and the early 1970s, the output was multiplied ten times over. In 1970, the peak-year, 290 reprint editions were published with 1.7 million copies. Table 3.7 provides information about the publications under this Program during the period from 1962 to 1988.

It is evident that after 1975, the Program declined to a great extent; especially during the 1980s, the number of editions reproduced is negligible. But the fact that during the past twenty-seven years, the Program brought out 12 million copies of American textbooks for the student community of India and made these books available to them at 1/5th of the American price is certainly its most valuable contribution to the country's academic life. It will be gratefully appreciated by all those who are concerned with higher education in India if the Program is revived in some form and more and more American textbooks are made available at affordable prices to the local student community.

7. SUMMARY

The above discussion should enable one to assess the U.S. role in developing library collections in India. In this task, both types of agencies, government as well as philanthropic organizations, have played an equally vital role. All these agencies were most active during the 1950s and the 1960s in providing grants to various institutions in India, and a few additional grants did come from the foundations during the 1970s also. Of the Government-sponsored programmes, the India Wheat Loan Educational Exchange Program concentrated mostly on the universities, though certain other research institutions were also provided grants for library development. The assistance was provided by way of grants for book purchases and journal subscriptions, arranging exchange of personnel, organizing workshops for librarians and setting up extension libraries. The second government-sponsored programme, viz. the Indo-American Technical Cooperation Program, assisted various types of other institutions, but the assistance came only in one form, i. e. book grants. The Program did not envisage either exchange of personnel (at least in the fields of librarianship) or organizing workshops for librarians. In the case of foundations, library development had in the nature of things never a high priority in their international programmes, but the grants provided by them indicate that they did take congnizance of as a vital sector in the total national development.

TABLE 3.7. Number of Editions and Copies Reproduced under the Joint Indo-American Textbook Program during the Years 1962-1988

Year	Number of Editions	Number of Copies
1962	19	49,000
1963	34	88,900
1964	75	383,871
1965	146	493,300
1966	153	658,100
1967	154	595,600
1968	124	596,452
1969	212	879,173
1970	297	1,679,906
1971	78	329,330
1972	289	1,390,019
1973	48	220,744
1974	51	172,002
1975	125	382,811
1976	39	183,129
1977	18	67,500
1978	7	23,275
1979	5	16,750
1980	7	23,000
1981	4	10,500
1982	1	2,000
1983	nil	—
1984	2	4,850
1985	32	—
1986	11	—
1987	35	—
1988	19	—
	Total:	12,000,000[80] (Approximately)

Lastly, it is worth noting that the availability of a large number of books on American literature and history prompted some Indian universities to introduce courses in those subjects at the post-graduate level. If the libraries of many universities and research institutions in India can claim to be adequately stocked today, the credit for providing the requisite momentum to their growth goes unquestionably to American generosity.

NOTES AND REFERENCES

1. Beverley J. Brewster, *American Overseas Library Technical Assistance,* 1940-1970, Metuchen (N. J.), 1976, p. 40.
2. India Government, *Report on the Indo-US Technical Cooperation Programme,* Delhi, 1959, p. 1.
3. *India Wheat Loan Educational Exchange Program*, Delhi, 1955, p. 2.
4. K. S. Deshpande, "The Wheat Loan Programme and its impact on the Indian library world," *Granthapal*, 4 (1962): 118-25.
5. A. K. Mukherjee, "Wheat Loan Educational Exchange Programme in India and the Indian university libraries," *Library Herald*, 6 (1963): 96-102.
6. Laurence J. Kipp and Cecilia R. Kipp, *Indian Libraries and the India Wheat Loan Educational Exchange Program—A report*, mimeographed, 1961.
7. *Ibid.*
8. *Ibid.*
9. Brewster, *op. cit.* p. 41.
10. S. Das Gupta, "A brief report on the visit to the United States of America under the India Wheat Loan Educational Exchange Program," *Journal of Indian Library Association*, 2 (1956-57): 27-47.
11. P. K. Banerjea, "American libraries as viewed by an Indian librarian," *Indian Librarian*, 12 (1957-58): 59-64.
12. Vidyut Khandwala, "My experience of an American university library," in *Development of Libraries in New India*, Delhi, 1965, pp. 227-33.
13. Deshpande, *op. cit.*
14. *Ibid.*
15. Kipp and Kipp, *op. cit.*
16. Mukherjee, *op. cit.*
17. Kipp and Kipp, *op. cit.*
18. B. B. Hungund, *Development of University Libraries in India*, M. Lib. Sc. dissertation, Bombay University, 1969.
19. *Wheat Loan Messenger*, June 1961, mimeographed.
20. *Ibid.*
21. Murari Lal Nagar, *Wheat Loan Messenger—Report of the Proceedings of the Fifth Wheat Loan Library Workshop*, Delhi, *March 5-9, 1962*, Delhi, 1963, p. 9.
22. *Ibid.*
23. Kipp and Kipp, *op. cit.*
24. Indian Council for Library Development, *A Union List of Learned American*

serials in Indian Libraries, Delhi, 1966, pp. 410.
25. Kipp and Kipp, *op. cit.*
26. S. S. Lal, "Punjab University extension library, Ludhiana on the march," *Indian Librarian*, 22 (1967-68): 138-42.
27. *Ibid.*
28. S. Gnanamuttu, "Madurai university library—A decade of progress," in *Madurai University Library—10th Anniversary Souvenir*, Madurai, 1968, pp. 1-5.
29. D. Chandran, "Madurai university library—Progress in ten years," *I.L.A. Bulletin*, 12 (1976): 193-97.
30. D. Chandran, *An Assessment of the Development of Madurai University Library*, M. Lib. Sc. dissertation, Mysore University, 1974.
31. India Government, *The Report of the University Education Commission*, 1948-49 Delhi, 1962, p. 2103.
32. Lal, *op. cit.*
33. Kipp and Kipp, *op.cit.*
34. S. Bashiruddin, "University libraries since independence," *Cultural Forum*, 9 (January-April 1967): 39-44.
35. Hungund, *op. cit.*
36. N. B. Inamdar and M. R. Riswadkar, "India," in *International Handbook of Contemporary Developments in Librarianship*, p. 192.
37. Bashiruddin, *op. cit.*
38. *Indo-American Technical Co-operation, 1952-56*, Delhi, p. 5. Year of publication is not mentioned.
39. All these details have been taken from *Indo-American Technical Co-operation, 1952-56.*
40. India Government (Ministry of Education), *Annual Report, 1955-56*, p. 20.
41. India Government (Ministry of Education and Scientific Research), *Annual Report 1957-58*, p. 38.
42. India Government (Ministry of Education), *Annual Report 1958-59*, p. 43.
43. Brewster, *op. cit.*, p. 103.
44. *Ibid.*, p. 120.
45. Carnegie Corporation's Letter dated 18 September, 1985 to the author.
46. Brewster, *op. cit.*, p. 121.
47. All these details have been taken from the Rockefeller Foundation's annual reports for the corresponding years.
48. Raymond B. Fosdick, *The Story of the Rockefeller Foundation: Nineteen Thirteen to Nineteen Fifty*, New York, 1952, p. 300.
49. Robert A. Mayer, "Ford Foundation," in *Encyclopedia of Library and Information Science*, Vol. 8, New York, 1972, pp. 592-600.
50. K. C. Naik and Sankaram, *A History of Agricultural Universities*, New Delhi, 1972, p. 114.
51. Ford Foundation, *The Ford Foundation and Foundation Supported Activities in India*, New Delhi, 1955, pp. 106.
52. Ford Foundation, *The Ford Foundation and Foundation Supported activities in India: Summary of Grants from 1951 to 1969*, New Delhi, p. 35, Year of publication is not mentioned.
53. C. D. Deshmukh, *The Course of My Life*, New Delhi, 1974, pp. 269-70.
54. University of Delhi, Delhi, Draft from the office records, Typescript.

55. Ford Foundation, *Summary of Grants*, *op. cit.*, p. 28.
56. *Ibid.*, p. 31.
57. Naik and Sankaram, *op. cit.*, p. 120.
58. Data have been collected from the Indian Council of Social Science Research Office, New Delhi, 21 May 1985.
59. *Ibid.*
60 *Ibid.*
61. *Ibid.*
62. Data have been collected from Dr. V. M. Dandekar, Director, Indian School of Political Economy, Lonavala, 13 September 1985.
63. Data have been collected from Dr. T. S. Papola, Director, Giri Institute of Development Studies, Lucknow, 9 May 1985.
64. Deccan College Post-Graduate and research Institute, Pune, Letter dated 26 September 1984 to the author.
65. Data have been collected from the Indian Council of Social Science Research office, New Delhi, 21 May 1985.
66. Sohan Singh, "Books Program of the Asia Foundation in India," *Timeless Fellowship*, 2 (1965): 61-64.
67. *Ibid.*
68. *Ibid.*
69. Asia Foundation's Letter dated 5 August 1983 to the author.
70. Sohan Singh, *op. cit.*
71. Juliane M. Heyman, "Asia Foundation libraries,' *Library Journal*, 82 (1957): 2890-92.
72. American Studies Research Centre, Hyderabad, letter dated 29 September 1983 to the author.
73. Asia Foundation, *op. cit.*
74. "News and information," *Indian Librarian*, 10 (1955-56): 126.
75. *Ibid.*, 14 (1959-60): 201.
76. *Ibid.*, 15 (1960-61): 83.
77. *Ibid.*, 7 (1952-53): 131-32.
78. Curtis G. Benjamin, *U.S. Books Abroad: Neglected Ambassadors*, Washington (D. C.), 1984, p. 30.
79. *Ibid.*, p. 30.
80. Figures for the years from 1962 to 1981 have been taken from U.S. Books Abroad-Neglected Ambassadors, p. 90. and those for the years from 1982 to 1988 have been collected from the American Center Library, New Delhi.

4

U.S. ROLE IN LIBRARY SCIENCE EDUCATION IN INDIA

1. INTRODUCTION

The United States also played a significant role in developing Indian librarianship by contributing to library science education in this country. Despite a claim that "provision for some sort of training in librarianship must have been in existence since time immemorial",[1] the first printed mention of training for librarianship is to be found in the proceedings of the meeting of the Library Association of the United Kingdom held in London in 1887[2], which proved germinal in the case of several American libraries represented at the meeting, resulting in the establishment of a school solely for professional training of librarians at Columbia College at New York in 1887. Columbia "is considered to be the first school of training for librarians in the world".[3]

Although books and libraries existed in India's historic past, the history of professional education for librarianship in India is of recent origin. The need for professionally qualified personnel to manage libraries was recognized only in the early decades of the present century and library education programmes were instituted at a few places even before independence.[4] In what follows, the U.S. contribution to the growth of library science education in India is reviewed from three points of view, viz. initiation of library science training by W. A. Borden and A. D. Dickinson, the work of American library specialists as visiting professors at Indian universities, and migration of Indian library professionals to the U.S. for advanced training or for doctoral work.

2. LIBRARY SCIENCE TRAINING BY W. A. BORDEN AND A. D. DICKINSON

Library training classes were started at Baroda (1910) by Borden and at Lahore (1915) by Dickinson. "Prior to this there was some sort of in-service training in library routines in some of the larger libraries, such as the university libraries established in the nineteenth century and also a mention in some reports of such training in the Imperial Library (now the National Library), organized by John Macfarlane, the first librarian of that library from 1901 to 1906".[5] However, "modern library education with emphasis on its two main streams of specialization in public and academic libraries was separately inaugurated in India by Borden and Dickinson".[6]

2.1 W. A. Borden

Education for librarianship was an integral part for Borden of his professional activity. Even as he left the U.S. for India, he had planned to start library training in Baroda. He knew that the success of any library service depended upon the supply of trained librarians and he therefore began a series of library classes. Having been associated as a teacher with the library school organized by Dewey, Borden introduced many of the characteristics of the Columbia library school into India through his system of training. Writing about his activity of library training in Baroda, Borden says:

> I began by selecting a class of ten men and women of exceptional ability and I gave them a thorough training in the theory and practice of librarianship. After they had one year of instruction and another year of practical work in the Central Library, I opened a Summer School for town librarians in Baroda city (1913), making the course of five months, and putting the members of original class as instructors.[7]

Obviously, Borden had two objectives: to produce librarians, and to prepare training personnel to multiply their number.

The first class was started on 6 March, 1911. The *Report on Public Instruction* for the year 1910-11 claimed that "nowhere in India has there been up to now a single library class attached to any of the libraries where young men and women could be trained in the most up-to-date requirements of library economy".[8] The duration of the course was one year during which "all the modern requirements of library administration such as accessioning, classifying and cataloguing, charging and discharging, and various other practical details were taught".[9]

Another class was opened in 1913 for training librarians for the town libraries in the districts. Twenty-one persons were admitted on a monthly scholarship of Rs. 20 and after a training of five months they were sent back to their libraries to take up systematic work.[10] However, an attempt in 1912 to start a two-year post-graduate diploma course at the Baroda College does not seem to have met with success. The training course in Baroda continued up to 1924.[11]

Systematic education for librarianship is thus an American gift to India, and Borden was the initiator of it.

2.2 A. D. Dickinson

Dickinson's assignment as University librarian at the Punjab University, Lahore, in 1915, specifically required him to teach modern library methods to the working librarians. Accordingly, he established the first library school in India. The training course was known as a course in 'Library science' instead of librarianship.[12] This was perhaps the first occurrence in India, and probably in the world, of the term 'library science'.

His first class consisted of thirty students drawn from the staff of the libraries of the University and the local colleges. Compared to the curriculum of Borden, the curriculum introduced by Dickinson was more ambitious and covered basic subjects such as classification, cataloguing, bibliography and book selection. Syllabi of different universities in India in library science education at the graduate levelstarted at Baroda (1910) by Borden and at Lahore (1915) by Dickinson. "Prior to this there was some sort of in-service training in library routines in some of the larger libraries, such as the university libraries established in the nineteenth century and also a mention in some reports of such training in the Imperial Library (now the National Library), organized by John Macfarlane, the first librarian of that library from 1901 to 1906".[5] However, "modern library education with emhis training course was "the forerunner of all the subsequent training courses and library schools established in India and held for a long time a place of pride among the library training institutions in India since it has contributed two National librarians namely, K. M. Asadullah and D. R. Kalia".[13]

2.3 Evaluation

The contribution of Borden and Dickinson in the field of library science education in India can be best summed up by saying that "as a result of the influence of these American library advisers, India decided in favour of educating her librarians through a professional school in preference to the system of apprenticeship then obtaining in the U. K. This policy has throughout been maintained in the history of library development in India. The first library school at the university level was established in the U. K. only in 1919. The Lahore library school is, therefore, considered to be the second in the world, the first being the Columbia school".[14]

3. AMERICAN LIBRARY SPECIALISTS AS VISITING PROFESSORS AT INDIAN UNIVERSITIES

Among the American library specialists assigned to India, three came exclusively to work as faculty members in the library science departments in Indian universities. Carl W. Hintz worked at the University of Rajasthan, Jaipur, during 1961, whereas Morris A. Gelfand and George S. Bonn worked at the University of Delhi during 1966 and 1968 respectively. Since their contribution is solely related to library science education in India, it is discussed in detail below.

3.1 Carl W. Hintz

Carl W. Hintz, University Librarian and Professor of Librarianship at the University of Oregon, Eugene, spent four months in 1961 (September-December) at the University of Rajasthan, Jaipur, as a visiting professor on Fulbright grant. During his stay at the University, he submitted to the Vice-Chancellor his recommendations for the development of the library in the form of about six memoranda.[15] No details of these recommendations are available. But what is relevant in the present context is that he studied the state of affairs of library science education in India and prepared a state-of-the-art report on it.[16] He made a detailed study of the syllabi of fifteen universities in India offering programmes of instruction in librarianship at the graduate level. This was the first comparative study of library science courses at different universities in India. It reveals the common content as well as significant variations in the combinations of subject matter. He also provided a list of books which were used for each individual paper. What is interesting is that in his conclusion, Hintz points out the similarities in the pattern of education for librarianship in India and in the U.S. Some of these similarities, according to him, are: the establishment of library schools, or departments of library science, as regular university departments at the graduate level; a trend toward upgrading the credential from a diploma to a bachelor's degree; and a move from part-time teaching by library staff to full-time faculty.[17] He also mentions the dissimilarities by pointing out the formal pedagogical method employed in India, namely, the use of the examination as virtually the sole determinant of the candidate's success or failure; and also greater emphasis put on the technical aspects of library operations and less on reference or service aspects. At the end, he remarks that:

> "the relationship between education for librarianship in India and in the United States is already evident, and hopefully will become stronger (since the exchange of visits of Indian and American librarians) is bound to affect the whole structure of librarianship."[18]

3.2 Morris A. Gelfand

In 1966, Morris A. Gelfand, Librarian and professor of Library Science, Queen's College, City University of New York, New York, was appointed professor for one-semester assignment (July-September) in the Department of Library Science at the University of Delhi. During his short stay in India, along with the teaching assignment, Gelfand also conducted an intensive and searching survey of the Department and submitted his report to the University.[19] As he himself stated, "The purpose of this report is to describe and evaluate the activities of the Department of Library Science in the light of its objectives, to offer suggestions for broadening the scope of the objectives, and improving the quality of performance and to identify problems and areas of concern which call for further study and sympathetic support. The report is based upon close to three months observation and participation in the work of the Department by the writer."[20]

Unlike the Carl White Report, the Gelfand Report has not been extensively reviewed. Only two reviews, one by Mangla and the other by Gupta, which provide a critical evaluation of it, are available.[21-22] Mangla admits that the report is not a comparative study as it deals with the functioning of only one department of library science; however, he believes that "as a case study, its contents should be of great value for other departments of library science in the country as a whole".

One of the most important recommendations by Gelfand is that M.

Lib. Sc. should be regarded as an intermediate research degree leading toward the Ph. D. This recommendation can be adequately validated by at least a couple of universities in India where the greater part of master's programme is devoted to research.

The Report has some shortcomings as no specific suggestion is found in it in connection with developing research programme in the department; however, Gelfand has tried to give a comprehensive account of various aspects of the department of library science at the University of Delhi which is not without value.

3.3 George S. Bonn

George S. Bonn from the graduate School of Library Studies, University of Hawaii, came to India in 1968 under the Rockefeller Foundation grant and was attached to the Department of Library Science of the University of Delhi as a visiting professor. On getting settled in Delhi, among the very first things he did was to visit libraries of all types to gain the first hand knowledge of the state of Indian libraries and to talk with working librarians about the state of library education in India as they saw it judging from recent products. The result is his state-of-the-art report on library education in India,[23] in which he discusses many aspects of library science education in India, such as the students, the teachers, the curriculum, evaluation of library school programmes and compares these aspects with their American counterparts. Kesavan observes that:

> "Prof. Bonn, whose tenure of visiting professorship in the Delhi University is a mighty piece of good fortune for the Department of Library Science, has contributed a very shrewd and understanding analysis on the state of library education in India."[24]

4. INDIAN LIBRARY PROFESSIONALS TO THE U.S. FOR ADVANCED TRAINING OR FOR DOCTORAL WORK

Foreign students have been coming to American library schools since 1887, when a Bavarian was in attendance during the second year of the school which Dewey established at Columbia.[25] The desirability of bringing library school students from India to the U.S. had been stressed by Ludington in 1946.[26]

It is difficult to ascertain the exact number of Indian librarians migrating to the U.S. for training in librarianship. Among available sources in this regard are the Rockefeller Foundation's *Directory of Fellowship Awards for the Years 1917-1950* which includes names of Indian librarians visiting the U.S. under the Rockefeller Foundation grant; the United States Educational Foundation in India's *Directory of Fulbright alumni (1966)* which includes names of Fulbright grantees in India in all fields including library science; and the United States Information Service's *Directory of Indians who have visited the United States (1967)*, though it covers only the Northern and Central parts of the country.

All these directories reveal that various agencies/organizations in the U.S. provided grants to Indian librarians for their training in the U.S. Chief among the agencies are U.S. Government (State Department), various foundations, United States Agency for International Development etc. A few librarians in India also visited the U.S. as private students with financial assistance from their own universities. Table 4.1 provides numbers according to sponsors of all Indian library professionals to the U.S.

TABLE 4.1: Indian Library Professionals Visiting the U.S. During 1948-1988

Agency/Organization providing financial assistance	Number of Indian library professionals
1. Fulbright grant	16
2. U.S. Foundations including U. N.	9
3. U.S. Government including State Department, International visitors and all U.S. Government visits other than those under USAID or Fulbright grants	10
4. Private students including those with financial assistance from their own universities	7
5. USAID	1
6. Government of India	1
7. Private including tourists, business and professional men	1
Total:	45 *

* Names are given in Appendix IX.

4.1 Fulbright Grants to Indian Library Professionals

At the end of the Second World War, the U.S.A. sold to its allies (and to some other countries) enormous stock of surplus property left overseas. Because payment for these could not be made in dollars, the U.S.A. took credits in local currency instead. Public Law 584, 79th Congress, approved on 1 August, 1946, and popularly known as the "Fulbright Act", is actually an amendment to the Surplus Act of 1944. Because of the financial assistance available under the Fulbright Program, it was possible for teachers and research workers from several countries to visit and study in the educational institutions in the U.S. It was also possible for their counterparts in the U.S to go abroad for academic purposes. Since its establishment, the Fulbright Program has sponsored more than 42,000 Americans pursuing studies in 110 foreign countries, and more than 78,000 foreign scholars in the U.S.[27]

The Fulbright Program became operational in India on 2 February, 1950, when Prime Minister Jawaharlal Nehru and U.S. Ambassador Loy Henderson signed an agreement establishing the U.S. Educational Foundation in India.[28] By 1975, some 5,000 Indians and Americans had exchanged visits. In the field of library science, twelve Indian library professionals were provided study grants and two were provided senior research grants under the Program.

4.2 Rockefeller Foundation's Grants to Indian Library Professionals

Various U.S. philanthropic organizations such as Asia, Carnegie, Ford and Rockefeller, were actively concerned with the education of librarians in many countries in Asia, Africa and Latin America. In the Indian context, three librarians, viz. N. M. Ketkar, S. Parthasarathy and J. S. Sharma, were provided grants by the Rockefeller Foundation to pursue studies in library science in the U.S. during the 1950s.

4.3 Asia Foundation's Grants to Indian Library Professionals

Travel grants make up a small part of the Asia Foundation's programme, but the foundation had occasionally supported to enable Asian delegates to attend international meetings concerned with educational and other fields within the range of its programme interests. So far as the Foundation's assistance to librarianship in India is concerned, "the Foundation was active in this field of assistance during the period of its work in India, which dates back to some thirty years. The Foundation did provide a limited number of fellowships over the years for graduate study in library science in the U.S., and probably assisted some in-country programs to upgrade librarianship.

Foundation support would have been provided through Indian institutions, i. e. universities and professional library associations".[29]

4.4 Indian Library Professionals Completing their Doctoral Work in the U.S.

So far as the doctoral work in library science is concerned, the University of Delhi started its programme in 1947 and the Andhra University instituted it in 1966. Presently eleven universities in India provide Ph. D. facilities in library science and fifty-two library professionals were awarded doctoral degrees by Indian universities during 1957-84.[30] Even so eight library professionals, namely J. S. Sharma, M. L. Nagar, R. N. Sharma, K. Umapathy, U. K. Tikku, Y. P. Dubey, C. P. Shukla and Chandraprabha completed their doctoral work in the U.S. Attempts to collect more details about doctoral work carried out by Indian library professionals in the U.S. were only partly successful. Table 4.2 provides these details.

TABLE 4.2: Doctoral Work in Library Science by Indians at the American Universities

Sr.No.	Name of the awardee	Topic of research	University	Year
1.	J. S. Sharma	Mahatma Gandhi: A descriptive bibliography	Michigan	1954
2.	C. P. Shukla	A study of the publications of the Government of India, with special reference to serial publications	Michigan	1953
3.	M. L. Nagar	Public library movement in Baroda, 1901-1949.	Columbia	1969
4.	Chandraprabha	Bibliometric study	Illinois	NA
5.	U. K. Tikku	NA	NA	NA
6.	K. S. Umapathy	NA	NA	NA
7.	R. N. Sharma	NA	NA	NA
8.	Y. P. Dubey	NA	NA	NA

NA—Information not available.

4.5 American Books on Library Science as "Prescribed Reading" in Library Schools in India

If the extent to which American books on different branches of library science are "prescribed reading" in the training courses in Indian universities could be considered as an indication of American influence, the situation is as follows.

All universities in India which conduct library and information science courses at the graduate and post-graduate levels were requested to send their syllabi. Of the forty-four universities conducting these courses, sixteen universities responded, which included the Universities of Banaras, Baroda, Bombay, Burdwan, Calcutta, Delhi, Gujarat, Jabalpur, Jadavpur, Madras, Mysore, Nagpur, Poona, Saurashtra and also the Shivaji (Kolhapur) and the Osmania (Hyderabad). An analysis of these syllabi reveals that in all eighty-three American books in different aspects of librarianship have been prescribed in these universities either as textbooks or books for additional reading. A subjectwise division of these books reveals that twenty-six books have been prescribed in library management, followed by thirteen each in library philosophy and cataloguing, eleven in reference service, eight in classification, six in information retrieval, four in communication and two in bibliography. It is clear that Indian library schools consider American management practice as the most advanced and therefore worth studying. Similarly, a preponderant number of universities use Anglo-American Cataloguing rules, almost to the exclusion of other cataloguing codes for instruction in cataloguing. For reference service, works by Margaret Hutchins, William A. Katz, Louis Shores, and Constance H. Winchell are prescribed as textbooks. This American influence in the library science curriculum in India is but one manifestation of the growing Indo-American relations in all academic spheres.

5. SUMMARY

The above discussion leads one to conclude that the U.S. has played a significant role in library science education in India by starting the first formal library science training classes in the early period of the present century; by sending specialists to work as faculty members in library science departments in some universities, and by extending financial assistance to deserving Indian library professionals to pursue higher studies in library science in the U.S. Burgess lists two aims that the U.S. hoped to see accomplished while offering assistance to provide education for librarianship abroad, viz. to establish education for library service permanently in a university setting at the graduate level and to prepare a generation of professional librarians who would move into posts of responsibility.[31] In the Indian context, it is gratifying to find that both the aims have been accomplished. "The leadership of the United States in developing library programs of service and technical efficiency as well as in setting high professional standards for library training has stimulated many of the newly developed countries to seek American aid and help in establishing more modern programs of library service in their own countries"[32] and India is no exception to this.

NOTES AND REFERENCES

1. J. S. Sharma, *The Substance of Library Science*, Bombay, 1965, p. 53.
2. S. R. Bhatia, "Training for librarianship," *Modern Librarian*, 4 (1933-34): 109-13.
3. P. C. Bose, "Training for librarianship in India," *Journal of the Indian Library Association*, 1 (April 1956): 30-34.
4. P. B. Mangla and C. P. Vashishth, "Library and information science education in India," *Journal of Library and Information Science*, 1 (1976): 127-60.
5. A. Neelameghan, "India, education for librarians and documentalists," in *Encyclopedia of library and Information Science*, Vol. 11, New York, 1974, pp. 312-49.
6. N. C. Chakravarty, "Librarianship in India," *I. L. A. Bulletin*, 4 (1968): 37-46.
7. W. A. Borden, "Baroda, India, and its libraries," *Library Journal*, 38 (1913): 659-63.
8. M. L. Nagar, *Public Library Movement in Baroda, 1901-1949*, A doctoral dissertation, New York, Columbia University, 1969.
9. *Ibid.*
10. J. S. Kudalkar, *The Baroda Library Movement*, Baroda, 1919, pp. 69-70.
11. Mangla and Vashishth, *op. cit.*
12. D. R. Kalia and J. C. Mehta, "The impact of recent developments on Indian libraries," in *International Librarianship*, London, 1972, pp. 49-53.
13. *Ibid.*
14. *Ibid.*
15. Pushpa Dhyani's letter dated 21 January 1984 to the author.
16. Carl W. Hintz, *Education for Librarianship in India*, Urbana, 1964, Mimeographed.
17. *Ibid.*
18. *Ibid.*
19. Morris A. Gelfand, *Survey of University of Delhi, Department of Library Science*, Delhi, 1976, Mimeographed. Also published in *I. L. A. Bulletin*, 3 (1967): 114-36.
20. *Ibid.*
21. P. B. Mangla, "Survey of University of Delhi, Department of Library Science

(1966) by Morris A. Gelfand–An evaluation," *I. L. A. Bulletin*, 3 (1967): 137-47.

22. R. K. Gupta, "A few more comments on Morris A. Gelfand's Survey of Delhi Library School," *I. L. A. Bulletin*, 4 (1968): 70-72.
23. George S. Bonn, "The state of library education in India," *Annals of Library Science and Documentation*, 15 (1968): 57-- 75.
24. B. S. Kesavan, "Editorial," *Annals of Library Science and Documentation*, 15 (1968): 53-55.
25. Edwin E. Williams and Ruth V. Noble, "Preliminary memoranda" to *Conference on International Cultural, Educational and Scientific Exchanges*, Chicago, 1947, pp. 134-43.
26. Flora B. Ludington, Reports on India, 1946, typescript.
27. Glen Fisher, *American Communication in a Global Society*, Norwood (N. J.), 1979, p. 20.
28. M. V. Kamath, *The United States and India 1776-1976*, Washington (D. C.), 1976, p. 187.
29. Asia Foundation in its letter dated 24 September 1984 to the author.
30. Dev Raj Sharma, "Doctoral degrees awarded by Indian Universities during 1957-1984 in library and information science," *CLIS Observer*, 2 (1985): 18-23.
31. Robert R. Burgess, "Education for librarianship–U.S. assistance," *Library Trends*, 20 (1972): 515-26.
32. Alice Lohrer and William Vernon Jackson, "Education and training of librarians in Asia, the Near East and Latin America," *Library Trends*, 8 (1959): 43-77.

5

LIBRARY OF CONGRESS PL 480 ACQUISITIONS PROGRAM

1. INDIAN COLLECTIONS IN AMERICA

1.1 INTRODUCTION

A major programme that is responsible for collection development in universities and other research institutions and, to some extent, in colleges in the U.S. with the addition of Indian material is the Library of Congress Public Law 480 Acquisitions Program (PL 480 Program). Strictly speaking, it was not the first or the only programme undertaken to develop Indian collections in American libraries as Indian collections appeared in American libraries right from the close of the eighteenth century. The beginning was made with the establishment of the Salem East India Marine Society in 1799, where the first collection of Indology was housed.[1] From that date onwards to the present date, the process of developing Indian collections in the U.S. had been going on continuously; the entire period of this procurement activity can be divided into three clear-cut divisions as (i) from the beginning of the 19th century to just prior to the Second World War, (ii) from the Second World War to the end of the 1950s and (iii) from the inception of the PL 480 Program to the present.[2]

1.2 Development

In the early days, Indian collections were developed in selected university and other research libraries in the U.S. as the universities, where chairs of Sanskrit had been established in the nineteenth century, put an emphasis on library collection in the fields of philology, Indian classical literature, ancient history, religion and philosophy. Libraries at Harvard, Yale, Johns Hopkins, Columbia and California universities and also some other libraries collected to a greater or lesser extent selectively what was available through the regular channels of the British and European trades.[3] However, after the Second World War it was through the singular efforts of W. Norman Brown that the Pennsylvania University began to have the first large-scale collections in all fields of Indian history and culture. This pioneering programme was followed in the 1950s by various universities such as California, Chicago, Cornell and Wisconsin.[4]

1.3 National Defence Education Act, 1958

In this connection, it would be necessary to refer to the National Defence Education Act of 1958 under the provisions of which three South Asia Language and Area Centers were established at California, Chicago and Pennsylvania. These Centers were charged with the responsibility of developing teaching and research in twelve Asian languages which were defined as "critical modern foreign languages" by the National Defence Education Act. Further, Universities of Cornell, Duke, Texas, Wisconsin and Michigan were added as the South Asia Centers, making a total of eight Centers.[5] The necessity for development of library collections in these "critical" languages was recognized by the U.S. Office of Education and funds were provided by the Federal Government enabling many Centers to acquire and service the specialized collections in these languages.

1.4 Conference on American Library Resources on Southern Asia, 1957

Prior to the operations of the PL 480 Program, one more event took place which ought to be mentioned, viz. the Conference on American Library Resources on Southern Asia, which was held at the Library of Congress in 1957. The Conference was jointly sponsored by the Library of Congress and the Committee on South Asia of the Association of Asian Studies. One of the most significant accomplishments of this Conference was the generation of the India Wheat Loan Educational Program under Public Law 82-48 for the acquisition of Indian publications. The Conference also recommended to the Federal Government that money be made available out of the Wheat Loan Interest Fund (India) for purchase of Indian publications for American libraries. As a follow-up action, a special procurement unit was established in New Delhi by the Library of Congress with the collaboration of the Ministry of Education, Government of India, to buy and ship government documents for research centres in the U.S.[6] Thus, a concerted beginning was made to bring Indian material into the U.S.

2. PL 480 PROGRAM: ORIGINS

A natural outgrowth of the Farmington Plan, the PL 480 Program is perhaps the most significant development in American librarianship in the years since the Second World War. It is a programme which carries out large-scale acquisitions from areas formerly poorly represented in American libraries and which includes as one of its essentials what is possibly the first centralized cataloguing programme on a national scale.[7] The purpose of the Program is primarily to increase the consumption of U.S. agricultural commodities in foreign countries and to improve the foreign relations of the U.S.[8]

The origins of the Program go back to 1954 when the Food for Peace Program was enacted. This Program made agricultural products which the U.S. had in excess available to needy countries. These agricultural commodities were made available usually by purchase in the currency of the country concerned. In some of these countries, the amount of money accruing to the credit of the U.S. from the sale of these products had built up to a considerable total. As a result of a certain amount of lobbying on the part of scholarly groups in the U.S., the basic legislation was amended to include Paragraph 104 N under which the Library of Congress has been authorized since 1958 to carry on programmes abroad for the acquisition of publications, called the PL 480 Program. The paragraph in question reads as follows:

> Notwithstanding any other provision of law the President may use or enter into agreements with foreign countries or international organizations to use foreign currencies including principal and interest from loan repayments which accrue in connection with sales of foreign currencies under the title for one or more of the following purposes:
>
> For financing under the direction of the Librarian of Congress in consultation with the National Science Foundation and other interested agencies–
>
> (1) programs outside the United States for the analysis and evaluation of foreign books, periodicals, and other materials to determine whether they would provide information of technical or scientific signicance in the United States, and whether such books, periodicals and other materials are of cultural or

educational significance;

(2) the registry, indexing, binding, reproduction, cataloging, abstracting, translating, and dissemination of books, periodicals, and related materials determined to have such significance; and

(3) the acquisition of such books, periodicals, and other materials and the deposit thereof in libraries and research centers in the United States specializing in the areas to which they relate.[9]

3. PL 480 PROGRAM: DEVELOPMENT

3.1 Legislation

The legislative amendment became effective in 1958 as a result of the interest primarily of the American Council of Learned Societies, the American Library Association, the Association of Research Libraries, and the Social Science Research Council. The leading spirit in putting this legislation through Congress was the former Secretary of the American Council of Learned Societies, Mortimer Graves. Largely through his efforts, this amendment, sponsored by Congressman Dingle of Michigan was included in the legislation.[10]

In 1961, a request was made for approval for establishment of the PL 480 Program in three countries, the United Arab Republic, Pakistan and India and it was approved in August of the same year. The total appropriation for the three countries was $ 400,000 in soft currencies and 36,500 in dollars.[11]

3.2 Survey Team to India and Pakistan

In November and December 1961, a survey team was sent out from the Library of Congress to India and Pakistan. The team consisted of Horace Poleman, Chief of the Library's Orientalia Division, and two other members of the library staff. The team had to work out an arrangement with the host governments and with the American embassies for administrative support of the Program and to make initial contacts with book dealers and attempt to recruit local staff.[12]

4. PL 480 PROGRAM: OPERATION IN INDIA

4.1 The Delhi Office

While the team was still surveying the situation in India and Pakistan, appointments of the American staff were made. John Charles Finzi was appointed to the office in India, situated at Delhi, which was to have the responsibility for Pakistan as well. John C. Crawford was to work as his assistant.[13]

The Program actually started in January 1962 and the first shipments were made at that time. The libraries receiving the publications numbered only eleven, including the Library of Congress, at the beginning. During the same year, the Program was expanded by increasing the number of recipient libraries from eleven to eighteen. At present, thirty one libraries are receiving publications from India.

4.2 The Bangalore Office

Early in 1966, the Library of Congress opened an office at Bangalore to broaden the range of acquisitions in South India and to improve the quality of materials acquired. The first of these goals was accomplished through visits to significant sources of publications in the southern states, the second through working closely with the dealers in the area. However, in the interest of centralization in the work, the Bangalore office was closed in March 1967.[14]

4.3 Extension to Nepal, Sri Lanka and Bangladesh

In 1966, the PL 480 Program was extended to Nepal. Though there is no separate office in Nepal, under a contract, the agent in Nepal supplies material to Delhi office. After preliminary cataloguing work is carried out at Delhi office, this material, along with other Indian material, is sent to participant libraries. In the next year, the Program was further expanded to cover Sri Lanka and in 1972 to Bangladesh. The same pattern holds more or less in these countries as well.

4.4 Staff

At the Delhi Office, there are some sixty local people and two Americans–the Director and a Deputy Director. The Deputy Director shoulders responsibility for selection, cataloguing and other processing, and for participant communication.

4.5 Acquisition Procedure

The Delhi office is responsible for the acquisition of the material, although the dealers actually procure most of the material for it. There are blanket order contracts with dealers in the country and they acquire all current material with the exception of certain specified categories. By current materials is meant materials published in the current year and the year preceding and which includes almost everything, which could conceivably be of research value, excluding such things as children's books, translations from a western language into an Oriental language, ephemeral material, reprints etc.[15]

The Program originally adopted somewhat of a vacuum approach leaving it to participants to reject unwanted material. Refinements in selection were made gradually starting with the option to exclude certain languages and to approve all serial subscriptions to the presently highly detailed subject and language profile which allows for over 1,000 choices. A computer is used to determine the distribution once the subject profile codes are assigned by the selection committee. In 1967, an individual library could expect to receive annually approximately 30,000 pieces from India. In fiscal 1988, the number of pieces from India received by the largest participant was 23,365 pieces.[16]

4.6 Accessions List: India

In an effort to make PL 480 receipts known and useful to as many scholars as possible, the Library of Congress decided in 1962 to prepare and publish *Accessions List* in the countries where the Program was in operation. Accordingly, the New Delhi office published the first volume of the *Accessions List: India* in 1962. In due course of time, that office assumed the responsibility for production of *Accessions Lists* for India, Nepal, Bangladesh, Sri Lanka and Southeast Asia.[17] Since January 1981, the *Accessions Lists* for Afghanistan, Bangladesh, India, Nepal, Pakistan and Sri Lanka have been combined into one and are published under the new title *Accessions List: South Asia*, which is published monthly.

The Accessions List: India included all the Indian publications which were acquired by the New Delhi office for distribution to the U.S. participants. During the year 1988, the *Accessions List: India* was mailed to 320 libraries in the U.S., 398 in India, 250 in Pakistan and 295 copies among the 37 other countries.[18] The Library of Congress was clearly succeeding in making Indian publications known to more and more people not only in the U.S. and India alone, but also in other parts of the world.

In the context of Indian libraries especially, the *Accessions List: India* (now *South Asia*) is of great importance for a variety of reasons. First, it serves as an up-to-date alternative to the *Indian National Bibliography* because the publication of the *Indian National Bibliography* is very irregular. Secondly, the *Accessions List* can be used in libraries as a cataloguing tool and also as a tool for providing bibliographical services. Writing about the *Accessions List: Pakistan* in 1968, M. Adil Usmani in his *Status of Bibliography in Pakistan* summarized its usefulness to bibliographers as follows:

> The selection of materials is quite comprehensive and includes publications of all the languages originating from Pakistan. In the absence of a current national bibliography of Pakistan, this is the best source at present for Pakistan publications.[19]

The same comment equally applies to India.

4.7 Micro-filming Unit

Until 1965, Indian newspapers were supplied to the participant libraries in bulk, as over a hundred newspaper titles were subscribed from South Asia. It caused the participant libraries to face the space problem acutely and, therefore, the need was felt to provide them microfilms of newspapers. With a grant from the Rockefeller Foundation in 1965, the New Delhi office could purchase microfilming equipment and also train an Indian technician in the U.S.[20] One more camera was added in 1969 and three microfiche cameras were later installed in 1978, 1983 and 1988 respectively.

Beginning in 1965 with the microfilming of newspapers in India, the project was expanded two years later to include Pakistani, Sinhalese and Nepali newspapers and also the official gazettes from all the four countries. In 1970, the New Delhi office began filming Indonesian newspapers and during 1981, these facilities were made available to the Middle East Program and were expanded to include newspapers and serials from Burma and Thailand. In 1983, microfiche production was increased by fiching materials from the Middle East, the Maldives, South Asia and Southeast Asia.[21] During the span of ten years from 1978 to 1988, the New Delhi office has sent a total of 108,390 microfiche to the Library of Congress. Presently, the office microfilms 218 newspapers and gazette titles.[22]

4.8 Serials-binding Programme

In 1967, a serials-binding programme was established in India and Pakistan. Under this, participants may elect to receive serial publications in bound volumes only. Service copies are sent to them for their immediate use, if they are requested.

5. ENGLISH-LANGUAGE PROGRAM

It was felt in 1964 that the publications procured under the PL 480 Program served to benefit only a limited group of libraries in the U.S. It was also felt that the smaller libraries over a wide geographical area should also benefit from the Program and hence the English-Language Program came into being. Under this programme, an attempt was made to secure "important" English language publications from different countries including India.

In addition to serial publications, important monographic works were also selected and distributed to 310 libraries in the U.S. These libraries were widely distributed in the U.S., ensuring at least one in every state. The libraries to which serial and other publications from India were sent included college libraries and public libraries having interest in Indology.

Ways in which the English-Language Program might contribute more effectively to the needs of college libraries were discussed at the Institute for Librarians on Non-Western Materials held at Earlham College, Richmond, Indiana, during 14-19 June, 1965, under the sponsorship of the Great Lakes Colleges Association.[23] So also, in an effort to determine the Program's effectiveness for distribution of selected English-language publications, the Overseas Operations Division in the Library of Congress sent questionnaires in 1969 to the 290 institutions participating in the Program as well as to twenty-four libraries receiving English-language publications. through their participation in one of the area programmes. Replies from 287 institutions indicated general satisfaction with the materials received.[24]

In 1985, the financing for the Program changed radically. The Special Foreign Currencies which had continued the funding originally made from PL 480 funds were exhausted. The Congress of the United States greatly increased the dollar appropriation to support the program. In addition, the participating libraries made dollar contributions to the Library of Congress Gift Funds and funding was received from interest on rupee funds reserved for the United States India Fund. The Fund was established on 7 January, 1987 by an Agreement between the Government of India and the U.S. Government on Educational, Cultural, and Scientific Cooperation. Expenditure is now authorized from the interest and the principal of the Fund. In 1985 and 1986, remaining balances of Special Foreign Currency Funds carried forward from previous years were also spent.[25]

6. PL 480 PROGRAM: IMPACT

Patterson suggests that in order to evaluate the impact of the PL 480 Program, time should be divided into Pre-PL 480 and Post-PL 480 periods.[26] She then narrates in brief the Pre-PL 480 period situation in the Chicago University. About the Program she observes that ". . . we can definitely consider this [as] the beginning of a new era in library acquisitions, processing and servicing so far as the South Asia is concerned."[27]

6.1 Areas of Impact

The impact of the Program can, according to Patterson, be viewed in terms of six different areas or problems, viz.

(i) Teaching and research program in the universities in the United States has been immeasurably strengthened with the increased library support which has become possible because of the PL 480 Acquisitions Program. Students are much more adequately and more realistically prepared.

(ii) The acquisitions program in general has been more effective since the burden of ordering from the developing countries has been entirely lifted from the shoulders of the participating libraries.

(iii) The participating libraries were forced to take a decision on the classification and location of the South Asian books by language versus dispersal by subject regardless of language. For example, books in Bengali on Bengali history were shelved with other books on Bengali history regardless of language. It made people aware that there were important things or potentially important things in these heretofore unnoticed languages.

(iv) Because of the procurement of books in a large quantity under the Program, the workload in the recipient libraries increased immensely. They also felt the space problem for shelving these receipts.

(v) The recipient libraries were able to offer greatly increased reference and bibliographic services since many more books procured could be put in their reference collection.

(vi) In the case of recipient libraries, the whole definition of the realm of the possible in regard to South Asia studies and acquisition of materials has been totally changed because of the Program. They could build a library program for the future in a perspective of twenty or thirty years ahead.

Over and above these specific areas of impact, one of the great impacts of the PL 480 Program is to expand one's consciousness of what exists, and to develop the collection in heretofore unimagined ways.[28]

6.2 Two Types of Impact

Williams talks of two types of impact of the PL 480 Program, viz. (a) impact on the recipient libraries and (b) impact on the countries from which material was procured.[29]

6.2.1 Impact on the Recipient Libraries: Williams feels that the Program permitted increased research by the users of the recipient libraries and it meant more secondary publications in English, which filter down to the colleges, junior colleges, down even to the primary schools. He further adds that the information from the materials received under the PL 480 Program gets down into literature and spreads an ever-widening ripple that affects people who never read or see a PL 480 item directly.[30] The second aspect of this impact is the area of cooperative cataloguing and, according to the best of his knowledge, this was the first true cooperative cataloguing project in the U.S. in which a group of libraries paid to have centralized cataloguing done.[31]

6.2.2 Impact on the Countries from which Material was Procured: Williams further feels that, first of all, there is an improved market for the publications which has had a significant effect on their own abilities to produce publications that otherwise they would not have been able to publish. The publications have fostered wider knowledge of their own country elsewhere, and this wider knowledge invariably leads to greater sympathy; the more understanding there is, the better in general the world situations are.[32]

Somewhat the same answer was given by Donald F. Jay when he was asked whether there has ever been observed in India, and particularly in the English language, any impact of the programme on the book publishing industry there. Jay observes, "there has been some such impact and I don't think it has been confined to India. . . this is all to the good, especially in the case of some of the older materials that have for many years been out of print. Now we have acquired a great deal in the way of reprinted scholarly publications. . . . When a publisher knows he can sell 310 copies of the reprint, especially if it is a fairly expensive item, he knows it is probably going to be worth his while".[33] Patterson supported Jay and said that "there are a very large number of things being reprinted in India and Pakistan and which are being sent and we are happy about this. A lot of the 19th century Sanskrit and Indological materials are turning up".[34]

7. PL 480 PROGRAM: RECIPIENT LIBRARIES' REACTIONS

In order to gather more information about the Program's impact, all the recipient libraries getting material from India were contacted through correspondence and were requested to communicate their reaction to the Program. Out of the thirty-one libraries contacted, only the following seven responded:

1. University of California, Berkeley.
2. Michigan State University.
3. University of Minnesota.
4. University of Missouri-Columbia.
5. University of Pennsylvania.
6. University of Rochester.
7. Yale University.

The following excerpts from the communications received from some of them highlight the usefulness of the programme to them:

7.1 University of California, Berkeley

Of considerable interest to the scholarly community served by research libraries is the Library of Congress acquisition and cataloguing program in New Delhi, India. The association of the University of California at Berkeley with the Library of Congress program in New Delhi goes back 26 years. . . . For two and a half decades, these programs have enriched research library collections and have supported important research and instructional programs in academic institutions across the country.

Scholars at Berkeley have benefited in several ways from the

Library of Congress program. . . Indian studies at Berkeley began in 1906 when a position to teach Sanskrit was established. By 1950 the research collection at Berkeley included strengths in Indian Government publications, history, Indic literature, classical Sanskrit and Hindi language. The Library of Congress program built upon this strength and added several hundred thousand commercial, academic, and official publications, plus 1,800 current journals, daily newspapers, maps and sound recordings. . . . The resource material has enhanced teaching and research in academic discipline as diverse as history, political science, economics, anthropology, language and literature, religion and philosophy, and music.

The South Asian materials at Berkeley are valuable at every level of our academic programs: undergraduate and graduate courses, as well as graduate and post-doctoral research. It has been said by our faculty that the books and journals often serve as critical preparatory and background information before a field researcher goes abroad for on-site work. In many cases, the assemblage of data at a University like Berkeley is more comprehensive, and hence of more utility, than in libraries and offices actually on site.

The South Asian book trade, although lively and productive, is very diverse and decentralized. The centralized acquisitions operations in New Delhi enable Berkeley and other major academic institutions in the U.S. to acquire books and journals economically. In many instances, it would be impossible to obtain these publications without a system such as the Library of Congress has organized. Due to print runs of only a small number of copies, a publication might well be unavailable before we in the United States even knew it existed.

We share our collections on South Asia with other libraries. In California, the University at Berkeley is recognized as the primary resource library for South Asian research. We share our resources with the eight University of California campuses, with Stanford University and with other research libraries through cooperative arrangements and inter-library loans. . . . Our success in building research collections on South Asia must be shared with the Library of Congress office in New Delhi[35].

7.2 Michigan State University

The PL 480 Acquisitions Program added significantly to the holdings of the Michigan State University Library, which without the Program would not have been developed in such detail or volume. Also, bibliographic advisory service of a highly specialized nature was developed and rendered as a result of the resources available to the Library. The availability of PL 480 materials encouraged faculty and post-doctoral research in several disciplines, including Communications, Economics, Education, Political Science, Sociology, and others. The availability, through the PL 480 Program, of current imprints from India encouraged the Library's Collection Development Policy to concentrate upon the acquisition of retrospective materials through the antiquarian book market.[36]

7.3 University of Missouri-Columbia

We joined the PL 480 Program in 1975 and our intake was very limited, but in a very short period we have built a very good collection on South Asia. Because of the PL 480 Program, we were able to use our own funds in buying books from other countries and pre-1975 publications from India that could not be obtained under the PL 480 Program. So also, because of the additions of books under the PL 480 Program, we were able to provide excellent bibliographic and reference service.[37]

7.4 University of Pennsylvania

The University of Pennsylvania has been a participant in the program since its inception in 1962. The library acquired all published material in India in all languages, including monographs, serials, maps, ephemera, etc. The introduction of the program has had a tremendous effect on the original collection. It has helped not only to augment the existing resources, but also to expand and keep them up to date.[38]

7.5 University of Rochester

The participation of the University of Rochester in the PL 480 Program began in 1975. From the very beginning, its participation in the Program was limited to three Indian languages–Hindi, Marathi and Sanskrit–and English language publications. The Program has had a significant impact on the collection development at the University. Although its faculty has consistently had several members doing research on one aspect or another of South Asia (history, anthropology, linguistics, art, etc.), the University would have been unable to build the strong core collection it has now with the funds then available. In addition, the University could develop a coordinated collection development program with the four neighbouring libraries in Western

New York State to establish jointly a comprehensive coverage of South Asian materials in the vernacular. So also, the University could build up a solid collection in Sanskrit.

The fact that the University now has a solid foundation for a library in South Asian subjects gives it the possibility–and the justification–to allocate the funds necessary to support ongoing coordinated acquisitions in the areas which have proved to be of interest to scholars and students. This would have probably not happened without PL 480 Program. There is a noticeable increase in reference and bibliographic service. Because of the Program, the University now has the tools to answer most of the reference queries. In general, the Program's impact has been very beneficial.[39]

7.6 Questionnaire by the Association of Research Libraries

It would be appropriate to mention here that sometime in 1969, a questionnaire was sent to the seventy-nine member libraries of the Association of Research Libraries. Replies were received from fifty-two libraries, which included forty-nine U.S. libraries. Of the forty-nine U.S. libraries, forty-one reported that they were participants in the PL 480 Program in some way. As Dudley states, "There was a good deal of agreement as to the advantages to libraries of the PL 480 Program. Nearly all of the participants mentioned one or more aspects of the following statement: the program allows libraries to get material which would otherwise be difficult or even impossible to get, to get it cheaply, to get it easily, and to get it quickly. In addition, several libraries mentioned the benefits of getting catalogue cards with the books, or having them available from LC and one library pointed out that the accessions lists constitute excellent (and in many cases the only) current national bibliographies for the various PL 480 countries."[40] The utility of the PL 480 Program to American research libraries is unmistakably clear. The survey finding was that "no library indicated a desire to terminate or even limit its participation in any PL 480 Program."[41]

8. PL 480 PROGRAM: DRAWBACKS

8.1 Indian View

It is but natural that such a programme which is quite large would have some drawbacks. Girja Kumar presents a typical Indian view that "there is a certain amount of wastage inherent in such an arrangement because of the indiscriminate purchase in bulk without consideration for the intrinsic content of each publication".[42] He further suggests that "the colossal expenditure incurred on the programme should rather have been utilized to build up (i) national depositories in the country and (ii) several centres abroad (not in the U.S. alone), equally distributed over the continents . . . India could have insisted that funds [should have been] provided from PL 480 sources for an equal number of depositories in India."[43]

Girja Kumar appears to be oblivious that so far as other countries are concerned, it is not the responsibility of the U.S. to build up depositories there.

8.2 American View

Kayastha points out the shortcomings of the Program, from an American point of view. These shortcomings are:

(i) Only current publications are acquired through the Program, and there is no provision in the legislation for acquiring earlier publications, facsimiles of manuscript materials, recordings, etc.

(ii) When the Program started in various countries in the 1960s, the participating American libraries were not prepared to handle such a massive amount of material. If one visits participating libraries, one hears many different stories about backlogs of books, participant's book selection criteria, and methods of handling unwanted material. The worst handled materials by quite a few libraries are those in non-western languages. Books and serials in these languages are shelved separately from the general classified collections in remote inaccessible regions and in separate buildings. Access to these materials is by finding their numbers in the *Accessions List* or by random browsing.

(iii) The non-western language material is not included so far in the *Annual Bibliography of Asian Studies*, nor does it get included in any other bibliographies and indexes. Therefore, if a non-participating library wants to borrow this material, it has to have a copy of the *Accessions Lists*.[44]

So far as the first point raised by Kayastha is concerned, it is difficult to go along with him. It is a fact that because of the PL 480 Program, several out-of-print titles were reprinted and supplied to the

U.S. participants. So far as the second and the third points are concerned, Kayastha indirectly emphasizes the importance of the *Accessions Lists* as finding lists. As mentioned earlier, the *Accessions Lists* are supplied to several hundred libraries in the world. The problem of checking several issues of *Accessions Lists* can be solved through computerization.

9. PL 480 PROGRAM: A FEW MORE FACTS

Before evaluating and summarizing the PL 480 Program and its operations in India, it will not be out of place to mention a few more facts which throw more light on these activities.

9.1 Field Directors' Conferences

Since the inception of the programme, the New Delhi office has organized five conferences of Field Directors as shown below:

First conference	March 12-16, 1965
Second conference	February 9-16, 1967
Third conference	March 10-12, 1971
Fourth conference	November 1-4, 1977
Fifth conference	March 25-29, 1985[45]

These conferences were attended, besides the Directors of Field offices, by Washington-based officials such as the Chief of Overseas Operations, heads of various other divisions, etc. During these conferences, the delegates discussed their experiences, participant requirements, acquisition trends, and local publishing scenes. They also reviewed possibilities of expanding programmes by including new interests and developments in their respective areas. Decisions for the future were taken to improve upon the service to the Library of Congress and other American libraries participating in the various acquisition programmes.[46]

9.2 The New Delhi Office Twentieth Anniversary

In 1982, the New Delhi office celebrated its twentieth anniversary with a photographic exhibit "Books Make a Difference: Twenty Years of the Library of Congress Through Indian Eyes", which was displayed in New Delhi, Bombay and Calcutta. The exhibit was jointly organized by the United States Information Agency and the New Delhi field office.[47]

9.3 Installation of Microcomputers in the New Delhi Office

A major highlight of the year 1983-84 in the New Delhi field office was the installation of three microcomputers and the implementation of the first phase of a project to provide machine-readable bibliographic data from the field office to the Library of Congress. Staff from the Library's Automated Systems Office travelled to New Delhi to coordinate installation of the equipment. By April 1984, the field office staff at New Delhi had keyed and shipped the first disk, which contained 150 bibliographic records.[48] Between April 1984 and September 1988, 36,264 records were keyed and sent to Washington.[49]

In conjunction with this effort, the New Delhi Overseas Cataloguing Project (NEWDOC) initiated a major component in India when the head of the South Asian Languages Section in the Descriptive Cataloguing Division in the Library of Congress travelled to New Delhi in February 1984 to lead training sessions in the preparation of work sheets for personal and corporate name authority records. The worksheets are transmitted to the Library of Congress for inclusion in the machine readable name authority data base.[50] These sessions led the field office staff at Delhi to prepare worksheets for personal and corporate name authority records independently and since May 1988, records submitted by New Delhi have been loaded without review of the descriptive cataloguing in Washington to the LC database. By the end of the fiscal year 1988, the New Delhi office had prepared 7,337 name authority records and 290 serial authority records.[51]

10. PL 480 PROGRAM: OVERALL EVALUATION AND SIGNIFICANCE

Despite its shortcomings and drawbacks stated above, one would agree with Patterson when she says that ". . . PL 480 Program has brought about a dramatic change in the picture of library support of South Asian research and teaching in the United States since 1962."[52] She adds, "we are getting close to approaching comprehensiveness in the acquisition of current materials from all four South Asian countries, in all major languages and for all humanistic and social science subject areas . . . In general, . . . I believe that the whole definition of the realm of the possible regarding South Asia studies and library support has been transformed by the PL 480 Program.[53] In its relatively short life, this programme has gone a considerable way toward demonstrating several things. These are:

(i) It has made it clear that it is possible to set up an office in a third world country, staffed largely by nationals of that country, who can acquire and ship a substantial proportion of the current publishing output of that country, or that region, which is of scholarly interest.

(ii) It has demonstrated that a regional office, staffed in this way, can produce valuable bibliographic tools in an area where there are inadequate national bibliographies, more particularly in India.

(iii) It demonstrated in the early years that centralized cataloguing, particularly for material in fifteen or twenty relative exotic languages, could be funded co-operatively by a group of libraries receiving the same material at the same time.

(iv) It provided essential experience to the staffs of the Library of Congress and other American libraries in a collaborative venture of substantial magnitude and helped create a climate in which even the bolder National Program for Acquisitions and Cataloguing could be conceived and operated with considerable confidence.[54]

While stressing the necessity of having South Asian collections in the American libraries, Patterson writes:

> I believe, and I act on that belief, that representation, in a selected number of North American research libraries, of research and teaching material from the South Asian sub-continent should be in close proportion to its importance in the world, its historical significance, its vast area and enormous population. Up to now, South Asia has not been adequately represented. The Subcontinent is many things: It is the site of one of the world's two most ancient continuous civilizations; it is strategically located contiguous with the Soviet Union, and with China, the other long-lived civilization; it is also strategically located in between the currently crucial Middle East (West Asia, as it is known in the subcontinent) and the potentially oil and mineral rich parts of coastal and island South East Asia. The subcontinent contains the world's largest democracy and after the largest Muslim State, Indonesia, it includes the next three largest concentrations of Muslims–two of them in the independent Islamic nations of Bangladesh (70 million) and Pakistan (50 million); India itself has 62 million of Muslims giving

it the second largest concentration of Muslims in South Asia. After China, with its 750 million, the subcontinent contains the second largest population in the world–an aggregate of 690 million in 1974, of a fifth of the world's people.
Historically, for one or another reason, the United States has tended to downplay the importance of South Asia. But in terms of economics, geopolitics, international relations, and even on purely humanitarian ground, we cannot go on ignoring it.[55]

That way, the PL 480 Program has been remarkably successful and deserves unstinted praise for bringing to American libraries great quantities of book materials that would not otherwise have been acquired by these libraries. The opinions and feelings of the academicians, scholars and research workers in the U.S. in the late 1960s can be best summed up in the words of Robert F. Byrnes, Distinguished Professor of History at Indiana University. He writes:

> American universities and institutions such as the New York Public Library and the Library of Congress have. . . created most impressive collections of research materials on other parts of the world. Thirty years ago, American scholars in most fields of foreign study had to go to Western European libraries and to other parts of the world even to begin their scholarly research. Now, however, in most areas of research and study, several American libraries possess collections in which research cannot only begin but can also be completed.[56]

More recently, Daniel J. Boorstin, former Librarian of Congress and other Library officials appeared before the House Sub-committee on Legislative Branch Appropriations on 27 February 1985 to present the Library's fiscal year 1986 budget request. While stressing that programmes for automation and acquisitions in South Asia required special attention that year, Boorstin said,

> The. . . area requiring special attention in this year's budget is the need to find replacement funding for acquisitions in India, a program vital to our nation's understanding of a vast area of the world which includes one-fifth of the global population. . . . Because of the critical importance of the materials we acquire through this program from India, Bangladesh, Nepal, Sri Lanka,

Thailand, Bhutan and the Maldives, we are requesting that this program be funded with U.S. dollars. I cannot emphasize enough the importance of this information gathering effort."[57]

It is hoped that a way would be found for the participating libraries to continue to receive Indian publications even after the local currency accumulations are eventually exhausted.

11. SUMMARY

The above account reveals the important contribution the Library of Congress has made through the PL 480 Program to librarianship in the U.S. as well as in India. The Program established its effectiveness and has enriched collections of U.S. participants by collecting material from India. This material might have been lost to scholarship had no facilities for immediate, on-the-spot acquisition existed. Several thousands of Indian publications have been made available to students, teachers and researchers in the U.S. These publications have enriched their outlook on and information about India. The recipient libraries in the U.S. are now equipped to provide better reference and bibliographic services to their clientele. So far as India is concerned, the book trade here has benefited to some extent. So also, because of the *Accessions List: South Asia* Indian publications have been brought to the notice of the academicians and research workers in many parts of the world.

NOTES AND REFERENCES

1. Ved P. Kayastha, "Development of Indian and other Soutn Asian collections in the United States," in *Indian Librarianship-Perspectives and Prospects*, New Delhi, 1981, pp. 286-307.
2. *Ibid.*
3. Maureen L. P. Patterson, "South Asian area studies and the library," *Library Quarterly*, 35 (1965): 223-34.
4. *Ibid.*
5. *Ibid.*
6. Ravindra N. Sharma, "Asian sources in American libraries," *Libri*, 34 (1984): 27-43.
7. Robert D. Stevens, "The Library of Congress Public Law 480 Program," *Library Resources and Technical Services*, 7 (1963): 176-88.
8. Susan Van Kamen, "Programs in support of international studies at the Center

for Research Libraries," in *Acquisition of Foreign Materials for U.S. Libraries*, Metuchen (N. J.), 1982, pp. 176-85.

9. Donald F. Jay, Paper presented at the Conference on "The impact of the Public Law 480 Program on overseas acquisitions by American libraries," held at Wisconsin Center, Madison, Wisconsin, 12 May 1967, Mimeographed.
10. *Ibid.*
11. *Ibid.*
12. *Ibid.*
13. *Ibid.*
14. *Annual Report of the Librarian of Congress for the Fiscal Year Ending June 30, 1967*, pp. 39-40.
15. Jay, *op. cit.*
16. John C. Crawford in his letter dated 28 April 1989 to the author.
17. *Annual Report of the Librarian of Congress for the Fiscal Year Ending September 30, 1980*, p. 60.
18. John C. Crawford in his letter dated 28 April 1989 to the author.
19. As quoted in the *Annual Report of the Librarian of Congress for the Fiscal Year Ending June 30, 1969*, p. 16.
20. *Annual Report of the Librarian of Congress for the Fiscal Year Ending June 30, 1965*, p. 26.
21. Data have been collected from the annual reports of the Librarian of Congress for the relevant years.
22. John C. Crawford in his letter dated 28 April 1989 to the author.
23. *Annual Report of the Librarian of Congress for the Fiscal Year Ending June 30, 1965*, p. 26.
24. *Annual Report of the Librarian of Congress for the Fiscal Year Ending June 30, 1969*, p. 17.
25. John C. Crawford in his letter dated 28 April 1989 to the author.
26. Maureen L. P. Patterson, Paper presented at the Conference on "The impact of the Public Law 480 Program on overseas acquisitions by American libraries" held at the Wisconsin Center, Madison, Wisconsin, 12 May 1967, Mimeographed.
27. *Ibid.*
28. *Ibid.*
29. Gordon Williams, Paper presented at the Conference on "The impact of the Public Law 480 Program on overseas acquisitions by American libraries" held at the Wisconsin Center, Madison, Wisconsin, 12 May 1967, Mimeographed.
30. *Ibid.*
31. *Ibid.*
32. *Ibid.*
33. Question period at the Conference on "The impact of the Public Law 480 Program on overseas acquisitions by American libraries" held at the Wisconsin Center, Madison, Wisconsin, 12 May 1967.
34. *Ibid.*
35. Joseph Rosenthal, *Statement on Behalf of the Association of Research Libraries before the Subcommittee on Legislative Branch Appropriations, U.S. House of Representatives, on Library of Congress Appropriations for fiscal year 1986*, 5 March 1985, Typescript.

36. Eugene deBenko in his letter dated 1 April 1985 to the author.
37. Murari L. Nagar in his letter dated 27 March 1985 to the author.
38. Kanta Bhatia in her letter dated 11 June 1985 to the author.
39. Datta S. Kharbas in his letter dated 17 May 1985 to the author.
40. Norman Dudley, "The blanket order, *Library Trends*, 18 (1969-70): 318-27.
41. *Ibid.*
42. Girja Kumar, "South Asian traditional studies and modern area studies: Their impact on libraries," in *International Cooperation in Orientalist Librarianship: Papers Presented at the Library Seminars 28th International Congress of Orientalists, Canberra, 6-12 January 1971*, Canberra, 1972, pp. 251-62.
43. *Ibid.*
44. Kayastha, *op. cit.*
45. E. Gene Smith in his letter dated 15 August 1985 to the author. The sixth conference was held in July 1987; however, it was not organized by the New Delhi office and hence is not included in the text.
46. *Ibid.*
47. *Annual Report of the Librarian of Congress for the Fiscal Year Ending September 30, 1984*, p. 63.
48. *Ibid.*, September 30, 1984, p. 63.
49. John C. Crawford in his letter dated 28 April 1989 to the author.
50. *Annual Report of the Librarian of Congress for the Fiscal Year Ending September 30, 1984*, p. 63.
51. Data have been supplied by the Library of Congress, New Delhi field office.
52. Maureen L. P. Patterson, "The South Asian PL 480 Library Program, 1962-1968," *Journal of Asian Studies*, 28 (1969): 743-54.
53. *Ibid.*
54. William S. Dix, "The Public Law 480 Program and the National Program for Acquisitions and Cataloging of the Library of Congress," in *Acquisitions from the Third World—Papers of the Ligue des Bibliotheques Europeennes de Recherche Seminar* 17-19 September 1973, London, 1975, pp. 159-76.
55. Maureen L. P. Patterson, "South Asia library development since 1957," in *South Asian library resources in North America: Papers from the Boston Conference*, 1974, As quoted by Kayastha, *op. cit.*
56. As quoted by Edmond L. Applebaum, 'Foreign acquisitions program of the Library of Congress," in *Acquisitions of Foreign Materials for U.S. Libraries*, Metuchen (N. J.), 1982, pp. 15-25.
57. *Library of Congress Information Bulletin*, 44 (1985): 57-58.

UNITED STATES INFORMATION SERVICE LIBRARIES, AMERICAN INSTITUTE OF INDIAN STUDIES AND AMERICAN STUDIES RESEARCH CENTRE, HYDERABAD

1. INTRODUCTION

The United States Information Service (USIS) libraries, the American Institute of Indian Studies (AIIS) centres in different parts of India and the American Studies Research Centre at Hyderabad have served Indian clientele to a large extent and have played a significant role in Indian society.

2. UNITED STATES INFORMATION SERVICE LIBRARIES

The United States Information Service (USIS) libraries, "the best show-windows of the United States", are libraries of the U.S. Government, propagating her foreign policy, achievements in scientific and cultural fields related to the American way of life and living, and form a large and complex system of libraries in the world.[1]

2.1 USIS Libraries: Origins

The origins of the USIS libraries go back to 1943, when, following the U.S.'s involvement in the Second World War, several agencies disseminating domestic information were consolidated into a new agency called Office of War Information (OWI), as a clearing house and coordinating agency for war-time news and information at home and abroad. A Library Liaison Unit was established on 15 January, 1943 by the OWI to advise on library matters and to provide information and help in its war information programmes. The first official library of OWI was established at London on 10 May, 1943; five more OWI libraries were established in 1944, one each at

Melbourne, Sydney, Wellington, Johannesburg and Bombay. Though the OWI was closed in 1945 with the end of the war, a new agency called 'International Information Cultural Affairs' was created under the Department of State in the same year to take over the charge of libraries maintained by OWI. In 1953, a new agency named 'United States Information Agency' (USIA) was created to take over the charge of all the library units under the Department of State. To organize and administer the functions of 'Information Centres', a local agency, United States Information Service (USIS), was established in each country and all the information centers were named United States Information Service libraries.[2]

2.2 USIS Libraries in India

At present, the USIS libraries function at four places in India, viz. Bombay, Calcutta, Delhi and Madras. The first official library of OWI was established at Bombay in 1944; however, the first American library (the USIS library) started functioning at Calcutta in April 1943 when the U.S. Government set up a reading room on the third floor of Tower House, near Calcutta's Dharamtala crossing, to dispense war information.[3] The New Delhi library was thrown open to the public in November 1946 and the Madras library started functioning in 1947.

These libraries are special purpose libraries with defined goals, defined audiences and collections targeted to further specific objectives, though they strive to emulate American public libraries in some basic ways, such as freedom of access, open shelves, an atmosphere of walk-in-hospitality, free loan of books etc. which are the outstanding American public library characteristics.[4]

2.3 USIS Libraries in India: Resources

2.3.1 Book Collections: Compared to the collections in other types of libraries, such as university or research libraries, the collections in the USIS libraries are small, as these libraries are supposed to be most selective in their collections which are to offer "balanced presentations of responsible and relevant currents of American thought–conservative as well as liberal."[5] Collections of the USIS libraries in India vary from 18,000 to 23,000. The library at Madras has about 18,000 books in its collection; whereas libraries at Bombay and Delhi possess approximately 20,000 volumes each and the collection of two libraries at Calcutta put together comes to about 23,000. The total collection in each of these libraries is always kept up-to-date by constant weeding of old editions and outdated titles and additions of new ones.

2.3.2 Periodicals: The number of periodicals received by these libraries varies from 320 to 420. The library at Madras receives 320 periodicals whereas that at Bombay gets 340 periodicals. The other two libraries at Delhi and Calcutta take in 400 and 420 periodicals respectively. All these libraries also receive five to seven American newspapers each. Most of the periodicals and all newspapers are received by air within a week or a fortnight of their release in the U.S. This is especially helpful for those who prepare for competitive examinations as the periodicals and newspapers on display provide them with information on current topics and latest development in various fields. In addition to the current issues of periodicals, backfiles of seventy-six learned journals are preserved at the Calcutta library, whereas backfiles of about seventy such periodicals are available at the Madras library in microform where researchers have easy access to them. Both the Calcutta and Delhi libraries maintain microfilm of the New York Times from 1957 to date.

2.3.3 Other Material: Of other material which is preserved, mention should be made of video cassettes which are maintained in all the four libraries, their number being 60 in Bombay, 200 in Calcutta, 150 in Delhi and 250 in Madras. All libraries possess equipment such as microfilm reader, microfiche reader etc. Microfilm-cum-microfiche reader printer is available at three places–Calcutta, Delhi and Madras, whereas the Bombay library has two photocopying machines and one video machine.

2.4 Readers' Services

It is only natural that for these libraries, which get latest material and are rich in their reference collections and where access or membership is not difficult, the membership should be quite large. And so it is. The library at Bombay has a membership of 32,000 whereas that at Calcutta comprises 21,000 city and 600 outstation borrowers. The libraries at Delhi and Madras have a membership of 24,000 and 17,000 respectively. In all these libraries, college and university students form a large part of the total membership, followed closely by government and political groups. The users of the library at New Delhi, for example, include officials from the President's office, Vice-President's office, Prime Minister's office, Union Ministers, high level government officials, judges of the Supreme Court, high court, prominent editors, journalists, eminent educationists and other professionals. So far as the student community is concerned, two-thirds of the total membership at Bombay and one-third at Delhi comprise of college and university students. At Madras, as many as 7,000 out of the total membership of 17,000 are college and university students and researchers. One reason for such a large membership of students is that several American authors in the field of social sciences are prescribed for study in Indian universities and the availability of books in these subjects is a great help to students.

Among the services provided by these libraries to their users, mention should be made of current awareness service, article alert, individual book promotion, subject profiles of prominent individuals, carrels for research workers, etc. A monthly list of *Recent Additions to American Libraries* is mailed to readers, to keep them informed of what has been newly acquired and is available with which of the four libraries.

The various types of services rendered by the USIS libraries in India to their members are, in a way, supplementing services provided by academic and research libraries in the country. To some extent, they also fill up the vacuum, at least in the metropolitan areas, created by the absence of a well-established public library system.

2.5 Conferences, Seminars Organized by the USIS Libraries

The USIS libraries frequently organize conferences, seminars, symposia etc.; a few such conferences, seminars organized by them during the previous few years are shown in Table 6.1.

2.6 Internship

A striking feature of the USIS libraries is the internship they provide to young, fresh, talented students of library science. Over three decades back, S. R. Ranganathan, then professor of library science at the University of Delhi, arranged with the American library to provide training for a few university students. Since requests for professional guidance kept coming in from several Indian libraries, a formal programme of internship was introduced at all the four USIS libraries in India. It was introduced at Calcutta in late 1960s, at Delhi in 1968 and at Madras in 1971.[6] It is limited to ranking, fresh library science graduates recommended by the heads of departments of library and information science of the universities in the area. The library at Calcutta has employed so far 102 interns; whereas the numbers of interns employed by the libraries at Delhi and Madras are 55 and 110 respectively.[7]

TABLE 6.1: Conferences, Seminars organized by the USIS Libraries

Library at	Conferences, seminars organized
Bombay	Entering the information age (Pune - June 1980) attended by Prof. F. W. Lancaster
	Information centers *vs.* libraries (Bombay - December 1983) attended by Prof. Miles M. Jackson.
Calcutta	AACR II workshop (September 1982)
	Workshop on information sources and services (December 1983)
	Sources of information in the social sciences (April 1984)
Delhi	Reference service—A commitment
	Reaching out—The library of the future
	Entering the information age (jointly sponsored by Delhi and Bombay libraries at Pune in June 1980)
Madras	Entering the information age (at Bangalore) and lecture discussion (at Madras)
	Workshop on AACR II in some cities of South India.

The training received by the interns helps to inculcate in them a "spirit of service" and stands them in good stead in their professional life. Though these interns may not be absorbed in the USIS libraries because of the limited number of positions, they secure good jobs elsewhere on the strength of their internship in the USIS libraries. During their internship, they are exposed to the latest practices and trends in library science and hence they can easily adapt to their new and, at times, challenging assignments. By providing internship, the USIS libraries in India are in a way complementing library science education in India.

2.7 USIS Libraries in India: An Evaluation

Henry James has compared the organization and functions of the USIS and British Council libraries by saying that "both libraries have the same aim, to win friends and influence people–the British concentrate on the first, the Americans on the second".[8] Through many facilities and efficient service offered in a relaxed and pleasant atmosphere, the USIS libraries have become a good friend to thousands at the places where they are situated and elsewhere. It is here, within their four walls, that many Indian readers make their first contact with the American principles of free dissemination of knowledge, which is the very basis of democratic education.

Recently, the USIA has decided to launch a new campaign to promote American books in foreign countries. Charles Z. Wick, USIS Director, announced at a meeting of the U.S. Books Abroad Task Force on 17 January, 1985, at the Library of Congress, several steps to strengthen the USIS book programmes. These steps are:

(i) Strengthening present budgets for translations and reprints of American books and facilitating increased copyright transactions;
(ii) Putting the United States "back on the map" via international book events, book fairs, and travelling book exhibits;
(iii) Expanding "to the million-book level" [American] support for transfers of donated books to needy students in developing countries; and
(iv) Supporting key institutions in their efforts to build up their collections of American studies.[9]

When applied to India, these steps will certainly help USIS libraries to function more effectively. Instead of being "neglected ambassadors", the American books will once again be "ambassadors of goodwill". Indian people's interest in the U.S. is vital to both the countries–India and U.S. The USIS libraries are striving for its furtherence.

3. AMERICAN INSTITUTE OF INDIAN STUDIES

The American Institute of Indian Studies (AIIS) was established in 1961 by a group of scholars involved in programmes of Indian studies at several U.S. universities. They were led by W. Norman Brown,

Professor of Sanskrit at the University of Pennsylvania, who brought a long-held dream to reality with the creation of a non-governmental organization to facilitate research on Indian culture and history. Beginning with the establishment of central offices in Philadelphia and Pune, regional centres were later opened in India at Calcutta, Madras and a research centre at Varanasi with the main administrative office situated at New Delhi. However, the Center for Art and Archaeology at Varanasi and the Archives and Research Center for Ethnomusicology established in 1982 at Pune and later transferred to New Delhi are noteworthy for their library facilities.

3.1 Center for Art and Archaeology, Varanasi

The Center is situated near the banks of the river Ganga in Ramnagar and is housed in a sprawling building that once used to be a dance hall and later the Chief Court House of the Maharaja of Benares. It offers unparalleled research facilities to scholars of art and archaeology from all parts of India, from member institutions in the U.S. and from all other parts of the world with a comprehensive and continually expanding archive, complemented by a carefully developed library.[10]

3.1.1 Photographic Archive: In the Photographic Archive of the Center, more than 84,000 photographs of South Asian buildings and sculptures as well as paintings, coins, and prehistoric antiquities are mounted and organized by date and provenance. The photographs are freely available for study at the Center and scholars may request personal copies of a reasonable number of prints without charge. The photo documentation system is one of the best systems in the country.[11]

3.1.2 Library: The library of the Center is regarded as one of the best libraries for research in Indian art and archaeology. It has in its collection over 21,000 volumes and provides an open-stack reference collection. Some of the rare collections in the library are: *Marshall Monuments of Sanchi; Photographic Records of Barabodur; Archaeological Survey Reports* etc.

3.1.3 Other Activities: The AIIS at Varanasi also collaborates in archaeological excavations, publishes and helps in the preparation of a large number of books, and itself conducts research projects. One of these projects is the publication of an *Encyclopaedia of Indian temple architecture*. When completed, the *Encyclopedia* will provide the most comprehensive textual and photographic reference literature on the subject. The Center is also engaged in another large project, viz. *A Gazetteer of Archaeological sites and monuments in India*. The Center is recognized by the Government of India as an academic research body and attracts a large number of scholars to its lectures, seminars, and its library and archives.[12]

3.1.4 Photographic Archival Collection on Indian Art and Architecture at the University of Pennsylvania: In this connection, it is worth mentioning that in order to facilitate the work of researchers and scholars in the U.S., the AIIS maintains the duplicate photographic archival collection on Indian art and architecture at the University of Pennsylvania. The first major collection of photographs was sent to the University in 1976. Meister's personal collection of approximately 5,000 photographs was reproduced, mounted and catalogued as a study collection. The second and most important archive was acquired in 1979 when the AIIS gifted to the University its duplicate file of the photographic archive of South Asian art and architecture. In July of that year, the University received the first shipment of 40 crates of 23,000 photographs and about, 3,000 slides from India and in October 1979, the American Institute of Indian Studies/University of Pennsylvania Archive was officially opened to the scholarly community. Since then, the total number of photographs at the University has reached the figure of nearly 61,635.[13]

3.2 Archives and Research Center for Ethnomusicology, New Delhi

If language is the key to the mind of a people, music is the key to their soul. A very interesting development at AIIS took place when archives and Research Center for Ethnomusicology (ARCE) was set up in India at Pune and Delhi in 1982 with funding from the Smithsonian Institution to support the AIIS's Indian operations. Funds were also made available to the AIIS by the Ford Foundation to purchase and import necessary equipment to achieve the goals of the Center, which are:

(i) to centralize and make available in India copies of research materials (field tapes, cassettes etc.) pertaining to Indian music collected by foreign scholars with due regard to the rights, concerns, and wishes of depositors and performing musicians.

This involves two processes as (a) the obtaining of copies (of field materials in the form of tapes, cassettes etc.) from scholars before their departure from India and (b) the return to India of copies of audio-visual materials relevant to Indian music which exist abroad;

(ii) to foster ethnomusicological research in India as the study of all types of music in their individual, social and cultural contexts;

(iii) to advise, assist and coordinate activities of American and other foreign scholars carrying out research in Indian music; and

(iv) to provide facilities to scholars for research, listening and transcription of materials housed in the archives.[14]

Though the ARCE was established with centres in both Pune and Delhi, all activities were gradually consolidated in Delhi to reduce operational costs and improve efficiency.[15]

3.2.1 Audio Visual Archive: Towards achieving these goals, the ARCE has set up an Audio Visual Archive for preserving Indian music in the form of audio and audio-visual cassettes and discs. The recordings consist of field recording collections and commercial recordings. The field recordings collection project is the most important part of the archives and forms its core. In this project are collected field recordings of research projects of scholars in ethnomusicology, anthropology, folklore, performing arts, and allied disciplines. There are seventy-seven such collections to date. Though it is difficult to list all of them here, a few can be cited by way of example. Ann Gold of Cornell University deposited eleven audio cassettes of recordings of "Biyavalo", a genre of wedding songs from Rajasthan. Todd Nardin deposited six audio cassettes of Hindustani classical music; whereas Daniel Karp deposited fourteen video tapes of recordings made as a part of his project on the use of *tabla* in various contexts ranging from the classical music to the concert state to folk and popular music. Sharon Lowen deposited four audio cassettes of *Odissi* dance music and two video cassettes of *Odissi* dance.[16] so far as the commercial recordings are concerned, their total number in the archives today is as follows:

12" phonodiscs	1128
10" phonodiscs	400
7" phonodiscs	798
Prerecorded cassettes	3052 [17]

The thrust of cataloguing activities in the recent years is on the development of databases on an IBM compatible system. The cataloguing for commercial recordings, books and published material is being done on the computer and it is expected that by 1990 all ARCE's holdings will be computerized.[18]

3.2.2 Reference Library: The audio visual Archive is supplemented by a reference library which has already acquired books on a range of relevant subjects with a focus on ethnomusicology and has, at present, a total collection of 6,550 books on various disciplines. The main subjects of interest are music, performing arts, folklore/folk literature and cultural anthropology. The library also holds books on other subjects like Religion (Rituals, Cults), Literature, Linguistics and general reference books.[19] It maintains an extensive periodical section, having forty-eight journals from India and abroad, on various subjects such as music, Indian music, performing arts, folklore, Asian studies, etc. and also nineteen journals of pertinent learned societies in India.[20]

The monographs and journals are backed by a large and systematic collection of clippings and cuttings. The Clippings Project is designed to locate and collect press-reports and clippings of ethnomusicological interest during the period from 1818 to the present day. These constitute the English as well as the regional language press–especially Marathi and Hindi.[21] About 150 journals, bibliographies, indexes and newspapers in English have been scanned for this purpose. Major English dailies are scanned regularly for adding to this collection. The clippings have proved to be an indispensable reference source for scholars.[22]

The other project, viz. the 78 r.p.m. Project, envisages the processing and documentation of old and rare 78. r.p.m. discs of Indian music. The preliminary work on this project is under way and the re-recording will begin soon. Special re-recording equipment has been purchased for this project, but has not been received as yet. Meanwhile, the Center has received a few collections of 78 r.p.m. discs as donations during the last few years.[23]

3.2.3 ARCE: Participation in the Library of Congress Special Foreign Currency Programme: The ARCE, as a part of the AIIS, is a participant in the Library of Congress Special Foreign Currency Program. It assists the Library of Congress (LC) in the acquisition of sound recording by reviewing available recordings and providing a recommendation and basic cataloguing information. In return, the LC provides the ARCE with Indian periodicals and books in the fields of music, folklore and cultural anthropology.[24]

3.2.4 ARCE: Organizing Seminars and Workshops: The ARCE also organizes and participates in international seminars and workshops in the field of ethnomusicology. It organized the first seminar-workshop on Documentation and Archiving in Ethnomusicology at Pune from 24th to 30th September, 1984 on an international level. The seminar-workshop was attended by experts from many parts of India, the U.S., Egypt and Indonesia. The seminar provided "a common platform for reputed members of the scholarly international community and for field workers an opportunity to air their problems and seek counsel–essential requisites for the expansion of ethnomusicological studies".[25] The volume of working papers of the seminar has been recently published in a mimeographed form.[26]

A second seminar entitled "Text, tone and tune" was held in Delhi in December 1986. The seminar sought to bring together scholars from India and abroad to discuss issues arising from the intersection of text and music in the culture with which they work. The papers presented at the seminar are to be published as a volume edited by Prof. Bonnie Wade.[27]

4. AMERICAN STUDIES RESEARCH CENTRE (ASRC), HYDERABAD

While the American Center libraries, which are run by the USIS, serve the general public, another library at Hyderabad has for over twenty years been promoting an unobtrusive but quiet scholarship by providing resources for academics.[28] This is the library of the American Studies Research Centre (ASRC) which was opened in Hyderabad in April 1964.

4.1 Establishment

A group of Indian scholars and teachers of American history and literature met their American colleagues at Mussoorie in 1962 at a seminar conducted by the United States Educational Foundation in India. The group recommended that, in view of the development of interest in American subjects among Indian scholars and the introduction of courses in American subjects in Indian universities, a research centre be established at some central location in India where scholarly research could be carried on. The choice fell on Hyderabad as the Centre's home because Osmania University introduced, in the year 1956-57, for the first time in India, a course in American literature as one of the options at the Master's degree level in English.[29] The Centre is a voluntary academic body registered as Indian society and is supported by annual grants from both the Indian and the American governments, gifts from foundations and individuals and membership fees from scholars and institutions that avail of its services.

4.2 Membership

The use of the Centre's facilities is restricted to its members who number about 2,800. The membership is of various types, such as membership for two, three or four years, life membership, corporate membership for colleges and universities and overseas membership. As has been pointed out by Vyas and as can be seen from the following table, the Centre's membership is increasing tremendously. Table 6.2 shows the increase in membership from 1975 to 1984. It will be observed that both the institutional and life membership have made rapid strides.

TABLE 6.2: ASRC's Membership during 1975-1984

Category	1975	1976	1977	1980	1984
Corporate Membership					
University	22	19	19	19	18
Colleges	10	15	10	10	39
Individual Membership					
Honorary	8	9	9	—	13
Life	27	59	88	325	924
Regular	1,281	1,394	1,462	1,995	1,532
Associate	7	159	202	232	222
Overseas	8	19	43	—	18
Total	1,363	1,674	1,833	2,581	2,766 [30]

4.3 Collection

The library has in its collection 1,37,081 books including 3,401 reference books. As Vyas states, "since its inception in April 1964, with a small display of three to four thousand books, the library has continued to grow towards its goal of acquiring a basic collection of Americana comprehensive enough to make a balanced interpretation of American history, life and institutions, and, at the same time, specialized enough to serve the needs of scholarly research".[31] The collection contains 12,735 bound volumes of periodicals, 5,074 vertical files, microfilms (1,146 books and 5,791 periodicals), microfiche (13,671 books and 3,524 periodicals), 134 records, ten cassettes, 188 VTRs etc. The Centre subscribes to 509 foreign and 88 Indian periodicals and receives 148 periodicals either in exchange or as gift. All this shows the comprehensiveness of the collections.[32]

4.4 Reader Services

Among the unique features of the services rendered to readers, mention should be made of postal circulation service, preparation of check-lists, photocopying and documentation services.

4.5 Evaluation

The ASRC's contribution to Indian academic community has been best summed up by Palmer who writes:

> American studies have not flourished in India, in spite of earnest efforts by U.S. governmental agencies and some American and Indian institutions and scholars. Most of the so-called programs in American studies that were established at several Indian universities have withered on the vine, and only a few, such as that at Bombay University, still hover on the verge of respectability. An oasis in the American studies desert exists in Hyderabad, in the American Studies Research Centre, which has by far the best collection in India of books and research materials on the United States (especially in history and literature) and provides excellent facilities and often generous support for Indian scholars who wish to carry on research at the Centre. It frequently organizes special seminars and other programmes in which Indians and Americans participate.[33]

The ASRC's activities speak for the role it plays in the Indian academic community. Amritjit Singh describes it as a kind of academic "ashram" for college and university teachers and points out that "it is unique, because it offers other Indian institutions a model to emulate in its courteous and efficient service to scholars from all corners of India".[34] In a way, as pointed out by John E. Reinhardt, the former Director of United States Information Communication Agency, the ASRC exemplifies the mutuality of global education. It not only contributes to significant research in American history, literature and society, but also "encourages expanded awareness of the world and meaningful identification with all mankind. The Center is unique in all Asia, since it epitomizes the basic concepts underlying an increasingly significant way of thinking about global education, and the growing mutual dependence among the nations of the world."[35]

5. SUMMARY

The American institutions considered in this chapter have played a vital role in Indian society. The USIS libraries have provided for India a model of public library service, served the student community in metropolitan areas and helped the country's academic libraries. They have in fact become an indispensable part of the Indian intelligentsia's world. By providing grants to American scholars to support their research on India, the AIIS has brought more and more of them to India. Its Centre for Art and Archaeology at Varanasi has provided inestimable help to scholars in the world for the study of Indian art and archaeology. The ARCE at Delhi, though in its infancy, is a unique centre of information on ethnomusicology. Conversely, the ASRC at Hyderabad provides a wealth of materials which would otherwise have been inaccessible to Indian research workers to study the totality of American society. Indeed, these American institutions in India are truly the harbingers of the growing Indo-American cultural fellowship.

NOTES AND REFERENCES

1. C. D. Sharma, "From other continents: A study of British and American libraries in India," *Lucknow Librarian*, 3 (1964): 65-81.
2. *Ibid.*
3. Manu Sahi, "American libraries in India," *Span*, 22 (March 1981): 10-13.
4. Joan Collett, "American libraries abroad: United States Information Agency activities," *Library Trends*, 20 (1971-72): 538-47.
5. *Ibid.*
6. The author could not get the information about the year in which the internship was introduced at the American Center, Bombay.

7. The author could not get the information about the total number of interns employed so far at the American Center, Bombay.
8. As quoted by Sharma, *op. cit.*
9. 'USIA plans campaign to extend the role of American books abroad," *Library of Congress Information Bulletin*, 44 (1985): 37-38.
10. *American Institute of Indian Studies*, A pamphlet, Year of publication not mentioned, pages not numbered.
11. *Ibid.*
12. Chidananda Das Gupta, "Scholarly pursuits in India—American Institute of Indian Studies," *Span* 26 (August 1983): 12-14.
13. John Mosteller, *University of Pennsylvania Indian Art and Architecture Photographic Archival Collection*, A paper presented at the meeting of the Association for Asian Studies, Mid Atlantic Region at Drew University, Madison (N. J.), on October 24-26, 1980, Typescript.
14. American Institute of Indian Studies, *Samvadi: ARCE Newsletter*, 1 (September 1984), p. 1.
15. American Institute of Indian Studies, *Biennial Report*, 1986-1988, p. 30.
16. American Institute of Indian Studies, *Quarterly Newsletter*, 21 (No. 2), 1988, p. 14.
17. *Ibid.*, *Biennial Report*, 1986-1988, p. 31.
18. *Ibid.*, pp. 31-32.
19. *Ibid.*, *Samvadi: ARCE Newsletter*, 1 (May 1985), p. 3.
20. *Ibid.*, pp. 3-4.
21. *Ibid.*, (September 1984), p. 2.
22. *Ibid.*, New Delhi, in its letter dated 17 May 1989 to the author.
23. *Ibid.*, *Samvadi: ARCE Newsletter*, 1 (Summer 1988), p. 2.
24. *Ibid.*, New Delhi, in its letter dated 17 May 1989 to the author.
25. *Ibid.*, *Samvadi: ARCE Newsletter*, 1 (May 1985), p. 1-2.
26. Ashok Ranade *et al. Work Papers from the Seminar and Workshop on Documentation and Archiving in Ethnomusicology, Pune, India, September 24-31*, 1984, New Delhi, AIIS, 1987, Mimeographed.
27. American Institute of Indian Studies, *Samvadi: ARCE Newsletter*, 1 (Summer 1988), pp. 1-2.
28. Sahi, *op. cit.*
29. S. D. Vyas, "American Studies research Centre Library," *Library Herald*, 20 (1982): 139-50.
30. Figures for the years 1975, 1976, 1977 and 1980 have been taken from Vyas, *Ibid.* and those for the year 1984 have been provided by the ASRC.
31. Vyas, *op. cit.*
32. All these figures pertain to the collection as on 8 August 1985 and were communicated by the ASRC in its letter dated 8 August 1985 to the author.
33. N. D. Palmer, *United States and India: Dimensions of Influence*, New York, 1984, p. 257.
34. Amritjit Singh, "An experiment in academic *ashram*: A close-range view of the American Studies Research Centre in Hyderabad, India," *International Educational and Cultural Exchange*, 20 (1977): 2-7.
35. American Center, Madras, "Ambassador Reinhardt dedicates new buildings of the American Studies Research Centre in Hyderabad," *Press Release*, 15 January 1979.

7

INDIAN IMPACT ON AMERICAN LIBRARIANSHIP

1. INTRODUCTION

In the bilateral library relations between India and the United States, as examined so far, it is apparent that the latter has almost always been the giver. The reasons for this situation are simple enough. First, it has been a partnership between a highly industrialized and affluent country on the one hand and a developing economy attempting to mobilize resources for development on the other hand. It was but natural that India's role had to be that of a beneficiary not being able to reciprocate materially. Secondly, it would have been scarcely otherwise in a partnership between one claiming highly developed librarianship and the other being on the threshold of the field. Such a reciprocal gesture was not required, either. India could make up in talent what it lacked in material resources, and contribute to the development of library and information services outside its own borders. This contribution, in the context of world librarianship, may be relatively small, but its worth is none too meager.

2. INDIA'S PROGRESS IN LIBRARIANSHIP SINCE 1950s

Since the 1950s India progressed rapidly in librarianship and this progress is noticeable in several aspects of the field. About fifty library schools were established in different universities in the country providing library and information science education at the graduate and post-graduate levels, twelve of which provided research facilities leading to Ph. D. Special libraries, said to be as good as anywhere in the world, came into existence in industrial organizations and research institutions. About twenty periodicals devoted to library and information science started publishing in different parts of the country. India was among the first to establish a national documentation centre as well as a national information system.[1] She now has a national informatics centre which has plans to modernize the country's library and information services and also has the capacity to exploit information technology for the necessary improvement in these services. Today, world databases in sciences are accessible to her academic community, spread over a hundred universities, through the National Centre for Science Information, Bangalore. A similar facility will very soon be available to her social scientists. Since the beginning of the 1970s she has been participating at the international level in information programmes such as INIS, AGRIS, DEVSIS and ISDS.

3. INDIAN IMPACT ON AMERICAN LIBRARY PRACTICES

As a result of this overall progress, India has provided a number of library experts to third world countries to establish library services, to operate the existing services and to impart education in library and information science. Many Indian librarians are currently employed in the western world including the U.S. However, since this study is restricted to bilateral relationship between India and the U.S., the scope of this account is limited to India's contribution to librarianship *vis-a-vis* the U.S. only. The present chapter seeks to explore the extent to which Indian impact is noticeable in American library practices.

To begin with, one would do well to remember in this context the cardinal difference in the development of librarianship in the U.S. and India. In its formative years, Indian librarianship was all but forged by a single person–S. R. Ranganathan. On the other hand, although there has been over the years, a galaxy of internationally renowned librarians in the U.S., none of them has influenced American librarianship in the manner which even remotely resembles Ranganathan's influence on Indian librarianship. From 1924 when he assumed charge as Librarian of the University of Madras until his death in 1972, India's contribution to world librarianship was made virtually by Ranganathan alone. Whether his ideas were considered acceptable or not, they could not be ignored by the library world. What follows is therefore mainly a review of the influence, such as it is, of the corpus of Ranganathan's work on American scholarship of the field.

3.1 Ranganathan's Impact on American Librarianship

Any person undertaking such an examination must of necessity appreciate that "one cannot, strictly speaking, discuss Ranganathan's contribution to American librarianship any more than his contribution to say, British or Canadian or any other country's librarianship. The seminal part of his writing is a contribution to library science *per se*, and as such, its ambit is universal."[2] Foskett in effect corroborates this remark when he calls Ranganathan an "internationalist."[3] Shera finds in Ranganathan one of the great figures of the present age in international librarianship and Carnovsky feels that Ranganathan exerted a profound influence far beyond the boundaries of his native land.[4-5] That library professionals from countries as widely scattered as the United Kingdom, the United States, German Democratic Republic, South Africa, Canada, China, Sri Lanka, Nepal, Yugoslovia, Pakistan participated in and presented their papers at the *International Conference on Ranganathan's Philosophy*, held at New Delhi in November 1985, only substantiates the views expressed above. Yet, the ideas which he propounded through his numerous writings on almost every aspect of library science and service caused differing reactions in different countries. Their acceptance, for instance, was more enthusiastic and more extensive in Great Britain while it was more restricted and far less obvious in the U.S.

3.1.1 Ranganathan and Classification in the U.S: Since Ranganathan is best remembered for his work in classification and cataloguing, it would be appropriate to examine the extent to which his ideas in these fields made an impact on American thinking. Library classification, as a matter of fact, had its beginning in the U.S. with the formulation of the Decimal Classification (DC) by Melvil Dewey in 1876. But, as every classifier knows, the DC is an enumerative classification scheme. And an enumerative classification scheme, again as every classifier knows, is incapable of yielding coextensive class numbers in many cases. This incapacity of the scheme "was seen to be due to the subjects presenting two or more free facets, whereas the scheme generally provided either for one free facet only, or for one frozen facet and only one free facet. This experience led to a vague feeling that a scheme for classification, suited to books embodying multi-faceted subjects, should provide for two or more free facets and not merely one".[6] This was the germinating cause which led to the formulation of the Colon Classification (CC) which is a fully free faceted, analytico-synthetic scheme of classification.

Colon Classification (CC), through its six editions, did attract attention of many American writers, such as Reparata, Merrill,

Gjelsness, Shera, Richmond, Atherton and Perreault.[7-13] Perhaps this is the only Indian publication in library and information science that got reviewed by so many American writers.

Despite this attention, the CC as a scheme for classifying books never succeeded in catching the imagination of American librarians. The main reason for this apathy, as noted by both Shera and Custer[14-15], is that an overwhelming majority of American librarians regard and value library classification as a merely utilitarian device for arranging books on the shelves.[16]

As a system of classification, CC's impact in the U.S. was therefore minuscule. However, it was the method of "facet analysis" that influenced them most and was duly acknowledged by them. True, as noted by Vickery and Garfield, certain aspects of facet analysis and synthesis had been anticipated to some degree in DC and even more in other classification systems, such as Universal Decimal Classification.[17-18] According to Shera, the great contribution of Ranganathan to this taxonomic world of library classification is that he began by thinking of what really goes on in the mind of a person while consulting a library file.[19] Ranganathan asked himself first, "How does knowledge arise?' and he said, "It arises in a variety of ways, by assembling, by coordinating and so on." This itself was something to which Ranganathan's contemporaries had not addressed themselves. Ranganathan realized that a book was not the same thing to all people. He began to think in terms of facets, talked about most favoured categories and determined his famous facet formula. This was a tremendous step forward.[20]

What is the relevance of facet analysis in modern librarianship? It has certainly not become outdated after Ranganathan's death in 1972. On the contrary, its importance is more and more recognized by all. Shera and Perry feel that it has opened the door for the introduction of electronic technology, popularly known as machine searching, for those who are seriously concerned with the retrieval of information.[21]

In stark contrast to the general apathy to classification in the American library world, a doctoral candidate at the Case Western Reserve University elected to study Ranganathan's influence on some special classifications designed in that country. Geraldine O. Matthews' dissertation is devoted to Ranganathan's influences on faceted classification.[22] She examines in the light of Ranganathan's technique of facet analysis three systems developed in the U.S. The first of these is the Encoding Telegraphic Abstracts developed by

J. Perry and associates wherein Matthews notices "many features in common with Ranganathan's system". "Both systems", Matthews observes, "overcome the rigidity of hierarchical classification, had inter-related facets, provided for new subjects, hospitality and emphasized the importance of the recognition of the three planes, idea, verbal and notational". However, she concludes that "Despite these features it was difficult to ascertain the extent to which the Encoding Telegraphic Abstracts (or SRU) system had been influenced by Ranganathan. However, the citation was identical:

> Actand
> Action
> Actor
> or Ranganathan's PMEST formula."[23]

The second system is a faceted classification for Physics of A. Herschman *et al.* (American Institute of Physics). In this, "the term facet classification was used and the citation order was not unlike Ranganathan's".

The third is that of the American Petroleum Institute's application of the technique of facet analysis to the organization of its subject authority list. The first seven of the nine facets from which the thesaurus terms were derived "were based on Ranganathan's PMEST formula inasmuch as they were entities". "This method", Matthews states, "which was similar to Ranganathan's was consciously applied to the 1966 edition (of API Thesaurus)."[24]

Later in her work, Matthews discusses the reasons for the rejection of Ranganathan's ideas, especially his idea of facet analysis of fundamental categories. Two principal reasons for rejection appear to be (i) the fixed number of five categories, and (ii) their predetermined or specified citation order.[25]

So also, as Vickery points out, if we turn to Lancaster's *Vocabulary Control for Information Retrieval*, we will find the term "facet" cropping up every so often. The book's final synopsis includes the following conclusion:

> A controlled vocabulary used for indexing must be synthetic; i. e. it must provide facilities for combining terms in order to be able to present any subject discussed in documents.[26]

To sum up, in the field of classification, CC, as a scheme, was virtually ignored in the U.S. However, even in the age of electronic technology, the concept of "facet analysis" has not failed to exercise those in that country who concern themselves with the intellectual organization of information.

3.1.2 Ranganathan and Cataloguing in the U.S: In the area of cataloguing, too, one finds little evidence of Ranganathan's influence in the U.S., the reason being that the dictionary catalogue reigns supreme in the U.S., whereas Ranganathan was a staunch advocate of the classified catalogue. In his study of Ranganathan's influence on the Anglo-American Cataloguing Rules (AACR), Agrawal points out that some of the rules of Classified Catalogue Code (CCC) were found incorporated in ALA Code of 1949 and he further claims that the influence of CCC on AACR (1967) is even greater and more visible.[27] This matter of 'influence' could be a debatable point. The adherents of ALA and AACR would be loth to admit that Ranganathan's theory of cataloguing and its product, CCC, really contained any guiding principles, other than those for rendering Indian names, as would affect the thinking that went into the formulation of those codes.

But it would be wrong to assume that the classified catalogue is totally unknown or non-existent in the U.S. "Classified catalogues are maintained by the John Crerar Library in Chicago, the Engineering Societies Library in New York, the Science-Technology Department of the Carnegie Library of Pittsburgh, and the Boston University Library."[28] The reason for the ubiquity of the dictionary catalogue in the U.S. is not far to seek. "The central factor in the success or failure of a classified catalogue is the efficacy of the system of classification upon which the catalogue is based."[29] The use of enumerative classification schemes such as the DC or the Library of Congress classification which are incapable of providing coextensive class numbers naturally inhibited the adoption of the classified catalogue in the U.S. "A classified catalogue demands of the classification on which it is based that it isolate specific subjects and synthesize such subjects as does the dictionary catalogue with its subject headings, for there must be no difference between the dictionary and classified catalogue in the ability of each to isolate specific subjects. This means that the classification system must provide coextensive class numbers for specific subjects just as the dictionary catalogue attempts to render them into specific subjects headings. To do this the classification system must be capable of development in such a way that it is able to describe a specific subject in terms of the notation just as readily as the dictionary catalogue can describe it in terms of verbal subject headings, and perhaps even with greater specificity. A synthetic classification is the only type of classification capable of meeting this requirement."[30] This is almost echoing Ranganathan.

3.1.3 Pre-Natal Classification and Cataloguing: Pre-natal classification and cataloguing was one concept which can be claimed as Ranganathan's direct contribution to American librarianship. About the nature of this concept and its utility to libraries, Ranganathan wrote in 1957 thus:

> The pre-natal classification and cataloguing of books, the release of catalogue cards along with the release of the books themselves, the printing of the call numbers in the books at the time of the printing of the preliminary pages, tooling them while casing the books. . . will make it possible for a library to release a book within not more than a couple of days of its receipt.[31]

After stating that the practice had not come into vogue anywhere before, Ranganathan made it clear that it was expounded by him in 1948 in an address at the Library of Congress.[32] In another article, he describes in detail how, in August 1948, he was called on to address a meeting of librarians at the Whittall Pavilion, wherein he said:

> We hope in India. . . to eliminate time lag of any kind. Before we can see whether it is practicable or not, *I want to give you that method* (stress this author's), so that the Library of Congress may experiment upon it and report to us about the possibility of it. Indeed, to put it in one word, we propose to practise pre-natal classification and cataloguing.[33]

It was on this principle of pre-natal cataloguing that, in June 1958, the Library of Congress introduced the Cataloguing-at-Source Project. It was a one-year project in which 158 publishers and 230 libraries participated.[34] In July 1971, the Library of Congress started the Cataloguing-in-Publication Project, which had its roots in Ranganathan's pre-natal cataloguing. Because Ranganathan had shown in pre-natal cataloguing how there would be national economy up to 79 per cent, the idea appealed to Americans. Pre-natal cataloguing thus could be considered an Indian gift to American librarianship.[35]

3.1.4 Five Laws of Library Science and American Librarianship: Although relegated to the last place for consideration here, *Five laws of library science* is in a real sense the progenitor of the entire gamut of Ranganathan's works. These laws, as he himself calls them elsewhere, are normative principles.[36] It is in the context of these principles that library practices and techniques assume meaning, and it is these laws which contain the implications of practices and techniques that may have to be devised in future. In the U.S., the *Laws*, like some other works of Ranganathan, did not invite much attention, so much so that its first edition went unnoticed by any American writer. In spite of its first citation in *Library quarterly* as early as in 1934, during the next five decades, it was cited only six times in American library literature.

There are nevertheless American writers–Shera, Garfield, Lancaster and Atherton being the most prominent among them–who recognize the *Laws* as an important contribution from Ranganathan. The very fact that Atherton chose to present an American view of these laws in her Sarada Ranganathan Lecture reveals the importance she attaches to them.[37] She states:

> Because these five statements have served as my guiding star throughout my professional library career, I would like to use them as the framework for my Sarada Ranganathan lectures.[38]

She avers that if Ranganathan had done nothing more than publish *The Five Laws of Library Science*, he would have to be seriously considered for a Library Hall of Fame.[39] Gorman, like Atherton, believes that, if for nothing else, Ranganathan deserves to be long remembered for his *Five Laws of Library Science* as these are the best summary of what libraries are, or should be about.[40] Garfield observes that the importance of these laws lies primarily in their emphasis on service to individual reader.[41] Lancaster goes a step further and demonstrates the relevance of these laws to the evaluation of library services and how they can guide decisions on what needs to be evaluated, by what criteria, and by what methods.[42] He further interprets these laws in the context of modern times by saying that in the long run, the acid test of "Books are for use" should be a test of cost-effectiveness; that "Every reader his book" can be considered a generic label that really means "Every reader his need"; that the significance of the third law is that a library should be evaluated in terms of its ability to inform people of the materials of potential use to them; that in the evaluation of library services the time of the user must be given sufficient weight and that the healthy growth of libraries implies adaptation to changing conditions and adaptation implies evaluation to determine what changes need to be made and how they may best be accomplished.

In another article, Lancaster focuses attention on the fifth law of library science and states that with the advent of a 'paperless society', library as a physical artifact may disappear, but the role of professional information specialist will not change much.[43] About the relevance of the fifth law in modern times, he writes:

> Were Ranganathan alive today, he would undoubtedly urge us to remember the fifth law. Most likely, he would point out that observance of this law is even more important now than it was fifty years ago. Furthermore, he would give us some leadership, point us in the direction in which we should be headed. There lies his greatness.[44]

3.1.5 Ranganathan's Influence on American Librarianship: An Evaluation: It should be clear from the foregoing that in the person of S. R. Ranganathan, India contributed a profound thinker to world librarianship. The ideas which he propounded through his writings on various aspects of librarianship, especially classification and cataloguing, did make some impact on American thinking in these fields. In classification, his pioneering role in making the concept of facets explicit has come to be widely acknowledged by American librarianship. In cataloguing, his advocacy of the classified catalogue as a tool superior to the dictionary catalogue in achieving rapid location of precisely pertinent material, and of the need of an analytico-synthetic scheme of classification to maximize the potentiality of such a catalogue found unqualified confirmation in the study undertaken by the John Crerar Library.[45] Five laws of library science were seen as embodying a philosophy of librarianship that harmonizes with the American concept of service.

3.1.6 Honours Bestowed upon Ranganathan by Americans: Compared to the profound influence which he exercised on British librarianship for almost a quarter century during the post-Second World War period, Ranganathan's influence on American librarianship has been much less visible.[46] However, that did not preclude American generosity from bestowing some of the most cherishable honours upon him.

The greatest ever tribute to Ranganathan came from the American Library Association (ALA) on his seventy-first birthday. American Library Association wrote to him, ". . . Most of us are not your disciples, all of us are your students, . . . we are proud to be in your debt."[47] In 1964, an honorary D. Litt. was conferred on him by the Pittsburgh University. One has to remember that only four people (including Ranganathan) were awarded the D. Litt. in 1964 by the Pittsburgh University, other distinguished recipients being Shannon, the father of information theory, Weaver, the man who first saw the possibility and worked out some of the early details of machine translation, and Quincy Mumford, the Librarian of Congress. In 1970, the Margaret Mann Citation was presented to him. That was the first occasion that the Citation was being presented to a person from outside the U.S. Ranganathan was cited for:

> his Colon Classification which has profoundly influenced modern classification theory and research through its faceted analysis techniques, for his works on the principles and structure of the classified and the dictionary catalog, and for a lifetime of signal devotion to the advance of library science.[48]

Recently, Garfield has clearly mentioned that, "We at ISI have fulfilled some ideas that are implicit, if not articulated, in Ranganathan's work. And I am happy to acknowledge the debt that all workers in classification and indexing owe this revolutionary thinker. . . . We acknowledged Ranganathan's contributions several years ago when we included his portrait in the mural at ISI entitled 'Cathedral of Man'.[49] The high regard which many American librarians personally had for Ranganathan can best be summed up in the words of Atherton:

> In time and space his work outdistances most;
> In personality he has no living equal;
> In energy he knows no limit, working past
>   the point of exhaustion for most;
> In matter, the scales would indicate great weight.[50]

3.2 Contribution of Other Indian Librarians to American Librarianship

P. N. Kaula, formerly University Librarian and Head of the Department of Library Science, Banaras Hindu University, Varanasi, visited the U.S. in 1968 at the invitation from the State Department of the U.S. Government. During this visit, Kaula delivered lectures at various library schools in several U.S. universities, viz. the University of Pittsburgh, University of Miami, the University of California at Los Angeles, Columbia University, Cleveland University, University of Maryland, Michigan University and Detroit University. His lectures covered topics such as comparative librarianship, comparative classification, comparative cataloguing and comparative library legislation.[51]

Except Ranganathan and Kaula, no other Indian library specialist got invited to visit the U.S. in the capacity of lecturer or consultant. However, a substantial number of Indian librarians are currently working in libraries in the U.S. Though it is difficult to ascertain their exact number, a few names are worth mentioning. Kanta Bhatia is working as South Asia Bibliographer at the University of Pennsylvania and Datta S. Kharbas as Head of the Asia Library at the University of Rochester. Murari Lal Nagar is Librarian of International Studies at the University of Missouri-Columbia and Ravindra N. Sharma is working as Assistant Director for Public Services at the University of Wisconsin at Oshkosh.[52] Though their contribution is hard to be individually assessed, one thing of which India can be legitimately proud is that the availability of Indian librarians to work as South Asia bibliographers in U.S. libraries has undoubtedly helped the Library of Congress to carry out its PL 480 Acquisitions Program in the most effective way.

4. CONCLUSION

In this relationship, it will have been seen that both India and the U.S. have contributed significantly to each other's benefit and a lot more can be achieved in future, too. To sum up in the words of Shera, "India and the United States can, and should learn from each other; each has its own contribution to make to librarianship. To India we can give our technical expertise, or machines, and for us there is the need for a rich philosophical tradition that Indian stands ready to provide. Certainly there is nothing new in such an exchange. The idea of international cooperation has been proposed many times and the resources for its implementation have long been at hand, if we will but use them. We can exchange publications,. . . can encourage visiting scholars,. . . exchange practitioners,. . . support teachers in our library schools to give instruction in each other's classes".[53]

Somewhat the same opinion was expressed by R. Thiagarajan, while suggesting possible areas of Indo-US cooperation. He states:

(a) First of all, India with its rich heritage in "knowledge organization and questioning" as evident in the Upnishads and other Sanskrit works, can contribute to a theoretical quest on the evolution of methodologies and techniques in "knowledge engineering. " But the refinement of such techniques depends largely upon the experiments to be conducted with hardware. This is where the U.S. information scientists could help. We could initiate joint projects between Indian and U.S. scientists on "knowledge engineering".

(b) Secondly, we must encourage more exchange visits between India and the U.S. for information scientists. This would enrich the work of both groups and help them mutually. While the U.S. side could give an exposure to the latest state-of-the-art to the Indian information scientists, India could offer a varied and complex scenario in "Knowledge engineering" based on Panini and other workers to the U.S. information scientists. At yet another forum also, I notice that in many of the Indo-US joint projects (including science and technology) scientists of other disciplines take a lead while the information scientists are relegated to the background. This has resulted in a total absence of projects and visits between the U.S. and India in information science and technology.

(c) The third area where U.S. and Indian scientists could cooperate is in organizing workshops, seminars etc. in various facets of information science and technology in the U.S. and India.[54]

So far as Indian contribution to library science is concerned, it has emanated from Ranganathan alone who was passionately concerned about library science not only in India, but in the entire world. He saw it as a vital tool for the development of mankind. To quote him:

Thus by the promotion of international co-operation in library science, the library profession will make its own contribution to the ultimate benefit of

1. the development of each of the nation of the world towards its own fulness at its own speed and along its own lines;
2. the development of an atmosphere of peaceful co-existence among nations; and
3. the evolution of One-World.

May Every Human Group Become Happy.[55]

NOTES AND REFERENCES

1. Indian National Scientific Documentation Centre (INSDOC) was established in 1952 and the National Information System in Science and Technology in India (NISSAT), a national plan which emerged from Dr. Peter Lazar's recommendations made to the Council of Scientific and Industrial Research, Government of India, to develop an information system on technology, was set up in 1975.
2. P. K. Garde in interview on 18 September, 1985.
3. D. J. Foskett, "Ranganathan's professionalism," in *S. R. Ranganathan 1892-1972*, London, 1974, pp. 23-25.
4. Jesse H. Shera, Review of S. R. Ranganathan's "Library books selection" and other books, *Library Quarterly*, 24 (1954): 255-57.
5. Leon Carnovsky, Review of "Library science today," ed. by P. N. Kaula, *Library Quarterly*, 35 (1965): 388.
6. For a detailed account of the genesis and development of the CC, see S. R. Ranganathan, *A Descriptive Account of the Colon Classification* (Bombay, Asia Publishing House, 1967), pp. 11-25. That book contains the proceedings of a seminar organized by the Rutgers University, New Brunswick, N. J. U.S.A., and was originally published in the "Rutgers Series on Systems for the Intellectual Organization of Information" by the Rutgers University Press. References cited here are to the Indian edition.
7. Mary Reparata, Review of "Colon Classification (1933)," *Library Quarterly*, 4 (1934): 501-04.
8. William S. Merrill, Review of "Colon Classification (1933)," *Library Journal*, 58 (1933): 782-83.
9. Rudolph Gjelsness, Review of "Colon Classification," 3rd ed., 1950, *Library Journal*, 76 (1951): 1798-99.
10. Jesse H. Shera, Review of "Colon Classification," 3rd ed., 1950, *Library Quarterly*, 22 (1952): 59-61.
11. Phyllis A. Richmond, Review of "Colon Classification," 6th ed., 1960, *Library Quarterly*, 32 (1962): 99-100.
12. Pauline Atherton, Review of "Colon Classification," *Library Journal*, 91 (1966): 1866-68.
13. Jean M. Perreault, Review of "Colon Classification," *Library Resources and Technical Services*, 11 (1967): 121-22.

14. Jesse H. Shera, review of "Colon Classification," 3rd ed., 1950, *op. cit.*
15. Benjamin A. Custer, Review of "Classification research," ed. by Pauline Atherton, *College and Research Libraries*, 27 (1966): 492.
16. In the Panel Discussion at the Rutgers Seminar, Mrs. Lea Bohnert was the lone American librarian who stoutly championed the CC and narrated how much she had benefited by using it to organize the reports and correspondence of the research and development laboratory where she was working. For her remarks, see *A Descriptive Account of the Colon Classification*, pp. 249-50.
17. B. C. Vickery, Review of "Prolegomena to library classification," 2nd ed., 1957, *Library Quarterly*, 28 (1958): 219-20.
18. Eugene Garfield, "A tribute to S. R. Ranganathan, the father of Indian library science," in New *Trends in International Librarianship*, New Delhi, 1984, pp. 263-79.
19. As quoted by S. R. Ranganathan in "Asia's contribution to library classification," *Ceylon Library Review*, 4 (1971): 11-24.
20. In the panel Discussion at the Rutgers Seminar, Shera was quite caustic in analyzing the American insensitivity to classification. For him, classification was "an intellectual discipline. " See *A Descriptive Account of the Colon Classification*, pp. 273-74.
21. Jesse Shera and James W. Perry, "Changing concepts of classification: Philosophical and educational implications," in *Library Science Today*, Bombay, 1965, pp. 37-48.
22. Geraldine O. Matthews, *The Influence of Ranganathan on Faceted Classification*, Ph. D. Dissertation, Case Western Reserve University, 1980.
23. *Ibid.*,
24. *Ibid.*, pp. 141-43.
25. *Ibid.*, p. 152.
26. B. C. Vickery, "Ranganathan's contribution to indexing," in *S. R. Ranganathan 1892-1972*, London, 1974, pp. 9-11.
27. S. S. Agrawal, "Ranganathan's influence on Anglo-American Cataloguing Rules," *Herald of Library Science*, 12 (1973): 171-75.
28. Jesse H. Shera and Margaret E. Egan, *The Classified Catalogue: Basic Principles and Practices*, Chicago, 1956, p. x, footnote 1.
29. *Ibid.*, p. 23.
30. *Ibid.*, p. 49.
31. S. R. Ranganathan, "Library science and scientific method," *Annals of Library Science*, 4 (1957): 19-32.
32. *Ibid.*
33. S. R. Ranganathan, "Pre-natal classification and cataloguing on its way," *Annals of Library Science*, 6 (1959): 113-25.
34. "Notes and News," *Herald of Library Science*, 24 (1985): 121.
35. After the dissertation on which this work is based was completed, M. N. Nagaraj, formerly Deputy Librarian of National Library, Calcutta, has drawn the present author's attention to the fact that proposals for Cataloguing-in-Publication were in fact made as long ago as in 1876 by Justin Winsor, then Librarian of the Harvard College, and by Henry B. Wheatley in his *How to Catalogue a Library* (London, Elliot Stock, 1889). This is incontrovertible evidence that Ranganathan was by no means the originator of the idea, but the

fact remains that he was propagating it before it actually materialised. The present author is indebted to Nagaraj for pointing out this lacuna in the research work.

36. S. R. Ranganathan, *Heading and Canons: Comparative Study of Five Catalogue Codes*, Madras, 1955, pp. 55-58.
37. Pauline A. Atherton, *Putting Knowledge to Work: An American View of Ranganathan's Five Laws of Library Science*, Delhi, 1973, pp. 158.
38. *Ibid*., pp. 36-37.
39. Pauline A. Atherton, "Dr. S. R. Ranganathan," *Library Resources and Technical Services*, 14 (1970): 582-84.
40. Michael Gorman, "Let us now praise—A reflective look at six persons who greatly influenced the art of cataloging," *American Libraries*, 11 (1980): 201-03.
41. Garfield, *op. cit.*
42. F.W. Lancaster and Rashmi Mehrotra, "Five laws of library science as a guide to the evaluation of library services," in *Perspectives in Library and Information Science (Viswanathan Festchrift)* Vol. 1, Lucknow, 1982, pp. 26-39.
43. F. W. Lancaster, "The library as a growing organism," in *Ranganathan's Philosophy: Assessment, Impact and Relevance*, Proceedings of the International conference organized by the Indian Library Association and co-sponsored by Sarada Ranganathan Endowment for Library Science, held at New Delhi, 11-14 November 1985, Delhi, 1986, pp. 51-53.
44. *Ibid.*
45. Shera and Egan, *op. cit.*
46. For Ranganathan's influence on classification activity in Great Britain, see Eric de Grolier, *A Study of General Categories Applicable to Classification and Coding in Documentation* (Paris, Unesco, 1962), pp. 94-100. By contrast, de Grolier's account of classification and coding activity in the U.S. (pp. 104-139) contains no reference to Ranganathan at all.
47. Cited by K. Guru Dutt in "The inwardness of Dr. Ranganathan," *Herald of Library Science*, 12 (1973):
48. "Awards and Citations, ALA, 1970," *Library Journal*, 95 (1970): 2636-37.
49. Garfield, *op. cit.*
50. Atherton, "Dr. S. R. Ranganathan," *op. cit.*
51. P. N. Kaula in interview on 17 January 1984.
52. Data about all these librarians have been collected from their letters to the present author during 1984-85.
53. Jesse H. Shera, "Of peacocks, elephants and the philosophy of librarianship," in *March of Library Science* (Kaula festschrift), New Delhi, 1979, pp. 19-25.
54. R. Thiagarajan in an interview on 26 April 1985.
55. S. R. Ranganathan, *Heading and Canons: Comparative Study of Five Catalogue Codes*, p. 281.

8

SUMMING UP

The preceding chapters illustrate the manner in which transnational library relations between India and the U.S. originated, developed and existed during the past seven decades. The relationship constitutes part and parcel of international librarianship embracing activities carried out between governmental agencies and non-governmental institutions and organizations, as also between individuals to promote, establish, maintain, develop and evaluate library, documentation and allied services in India and to foster librarianship and library profession generally in these two countries. It has been a relationship between two dissimilar library situations with one operating a highly sophisticated form of service, while the other being only a beginner. Naturally, much flowed from the U.S. to India. The present study has concentrated on this aspect by describing, rather at length, the role played by the U.S. in India in various ways: (a) American library specialists came to India to work in various capacities; (b) substantial U.S. financial aid was provided to several institutions in India by both governmental and non-governmental organizations including the foundations; (c) in the early decades of the present century, education for librarianship was introduced in India and later during the sixties, seventies and eighties, Indian librarians were provided financial support to study in the U.S. ; (d) Library of Congress PL 480 Acquisitions Program has been operated to provide thousands of Indian publications of research value to academic and research institutions in the U.S. ; (e) USIS and other American research libraries have been supplementing library services to Indian clientele.

1. OVERVIEW

1.1 American Library Specialists assigned to India

The earliest example of an American library specialist coming to India was in the first decade of the present century, when W. A. Borden was appointed as the first Director of the Library Department of the Baroda

State. Since then, a large number of American library specialists have come to India in various capacities. Their contribution to Indian librarianship can be measured in a number of ways:

(a) The foundation of a state-wide public library system in the Baroda State was laid by Borden. It was the first ever public library network in India.

(b) How public library service can be enriched by the introduction of mobile libraries, children's libraries and audio-visual aids was very effectively demonstrated by Borden at Baroda.

(c) The first professional library journal in India, *The Library Miscellany*, was launched by Borden. Library workers in the Baroda State required a forum to continue their education. *The Library Miscellany* provided that forum.

(d) What Borden did at Baroda in the matter of public library service, A. D. Dickinson did in Punjab in the sphere of academic library service. He laid the foundation of university librarianship in India. His *Panjab Library Primer* was the first manual of its kind to be published in India. Again, it was Dickinson who introduced university-based education for librarianship in India. The credit for the introduction in this country of open access and the DDC also belongs to him.

(e) The White Report offered the first self-evaluation model to University librarians in India. It demonstrated what a university library ought to be.

(f) American library specialists, while working as consultants at different institutions in India, prepared reports on the working of libraries at these institutions. Exemplary among them are those by Ralph Shaw, Dorothy Parker and Don Jett. These reports proved of immense help not only to the concerned institutions but also to Indian librarianship as a whole.

(g) Lectures delivered by American library specialists at different institutions in India, particularly at DRTC, Bangalore, acquainted Indian librarianship with new ideas and concepts in American librarianship.

1.2 U.S. Role in Library Collection Development in India

Another way in which the U.S. contributed to Indian librarianship was by providing substantial grants to institutions to develop their library collections. Several institutions in India benefited through these grants from a variety of U.S. sources–India Wheat Loan Educational Exchange Program, Indo-American Technical Cooperation Program, Ford Foundation, Rockefeller Foundation and Asia Foundation.

(a) The India Wheat Loan Educational Exchange Program was the largest and most complex U.S. aid programme involving university development in India during the 1950s. The aid came by way of funding for library collection development, providing opportunity to Indian librarians to visit the U.S. to observe the working of major libraries there, organizing workshops for librarians and helping in the establishment of extension libraries.

(b) So far as the Indo-American Technical Co-operation Program is concerned, it was not as wide in its coverage as the Wheat Loan Program. Though the Program did not directly cover the field of librarianship, it has nevertheless helped many institutions in India to develop their library collections.

(c) Alongwith the above-mentioned Government sponsored Programmes, non-governmental organizations, especially foundations, too, have played an important role in library collection development in India.

(i) The Rockefeller Foundation provided financial assistance to institutions as well as individuals in the field of library and information science. The institutions included universities, academic and research institutions in agriculture, medicine and home science, and a few other institutions. Grants to individuals were mainly for visiting libraries in other countries in pursuance of their current interests.

(ii) Although support for library development in India was not the principal programme thrust of the Ford Foundation, grants made by it to institutions allowed peripheral support for their library development. During the 1980s, many institutions conducting research in social sciences spent large amounts from the foundation grants for the development of their libraries.

(iii) The Asia Foundation played a major role in augmenting institutional collections. Universities, colleges and even secondary and elementary schools in the country received books through its "Books for Asian Students Program".

(d) So also, many institutions in India, especially universities, availed themselves of the facilities provided by the Universal Serials and Book Exchange, formerly the United States Book Exchange, which provided for the cooperative exchange of duplicates and other publications between libraries throughout the world.

(e) Further, it was because of the Joint Indo-American Text-book Program that nearly two thousand American university and polytechnic textbooks were reprinted in India and made available to Indian students at one-fifth of the U.S. list prices.

Thus, in the development of institutional library collections, both the U.S. Government and American foundations have played equally important roles. Without their aid, libraries of many an Indian institution would have remained much smaller in size and less rich in substance.

1.3 U.S. Role in Library Science Education in India

In library science education in India, the U.S. played a threefold role, viz.

(i) library science training classes were conducted by American library specialists in India in the pre-independence period,

(ii) American library specialists worked as visiting professors at Indian universities, and

(iii) the U.S. Government or the American foundations provided financial support to Indian librarians for visiting the U.S. for higher education including doctoral research.

W. A. Borden and A. D. Dickinson started library science training classes at Baroda (1910) and Lahore (1915) respectively, and, in doing so, brought to India modern library education with emphasis on its two main streams of specialization in public librarianship and academic librarianship. Borden had two objectives in mind, viz. (i) to produce qualified librarians and (ii) to prepare key personnel to multiply their numbers. He succeeded in accomplishing both the objectives. This was the beginning of library training in India.

The curriculum introduced by Dickinson at the Punjab University covered basic subjects in library science, viz. classification, cataloguing, bibliography and book selection. Dickinson's pattern is still continued in library schools in India as somewhat the same courses are taught even today. It was because of Dickinson's initiative in this respect at Lahore that India decided in favour of educating her librarians through library schools in universities.

Three American library specialists–Carl W. Hintz, Morris A. Gelfand and George S. Bonn–visited India exclusively to work in the library science departments in Indian universities. Hintz studied the syllabi of fifteen universities in India offering programmes of instruction in librarianship at the graduate level and in the process produced the first comparative study of library science courses at different universities in India. Both Gelfand and Bonn worked in the Department of Library Science at the University of Delhi. Along with teaching, Gelfand also conducted an intensive and searching survey of the Department and submitted his report to the University, whereas Bonn presented a state-of-the-art report on library education in India.

In the matter of library science literature, Indian reliance on American literature is fairly extensive particularly in the case of recent textbooks.

1.4 Library of Congress PL 480 Acquisitions Program

Though the Library of Congress PL 480 acquisitions Program is the most comprehensive of all in strengthening American library resources with Indian material, it is in no way the first and the only programme undertaken in this respect, as seizeable Indian collections appeared in American libraries right from the close of the 18th century. However, as a natural outgrowth of the Farmington Plan, the PL 480 Program is perhaps the most significant development in American librarianship in the years since the Second World War, as it carries out large scale acquisitions from areas formerly poorly represented in American libraries. At present thirty-one libraries are receiving publications from India.

The Program has two types of impact, viz. (a) impact on the recipient libraries and (b) impact on the countries (in this context, India) from which the material was procured. So far as the former is concerned, the Program enriched collections of U.S. participants, since several thousands of Indian publications were added therein. These are available to students, teachers and researchers in the U.S., and have enriched their outlook on and information about India. So also, the recipient libraries could provide better reference and bibliographic services to their clientele. So far as the second type of impact is concerned, the book trade in India has benefited to some extent as there is an improved market for Indian publications. So also, because of the *Accessions List: South Asia*; Indian publications are brought to the notice of the academicians and research workers not only in the U.S. and India, but also in some other parts of the world.

1.5 USIS Libraries, American Institute of Indian Studies and American Studies Research Centre, Hyderabad

The USIS libraries, the American Institute of Indian Studies centres in India as well as the American Studies Research Centre at Hyderabad, are taken as components of library relations between the U.S. and India insofar as all of them have served Indian clientele to a large extent and have played a significant role in Indian society.

1.5.1 USIS Libraries: With a variety of services rendered to their clientele, the USIS libraries in India supplement the services provided by academic and research libraries in the country. To a considerable extent, they fill up the vacuum, at least in the metropolitan areas, created by the absence of a well established public library system. By providing internship to ranking, fresh library science graduates, the USIS libraries also indirectly complement library science education in India.

1.5.2 American Institute of Indian Studies: While awarding fellowships to support scholarly research on India remains the Institute's principal activity, it also ensures continued exchange of scholars and scholarships between India and the U.S. Out of the five centres of the AIIS in India, two, namely those at Varanasi and New Delhi, are known for their library facilities. With more than 87,000 photographs in its collection, the Center at Varanasi serves the research needs of scholars in art and archaeology. The Archives and Research Centre for Ethnomusicology at New Delhi has set up a Sound Archive for preserving Indian music in the form of audio and audio-visual cassettes and discs. The sound Archive is supplemented by a reference library with books on a wide range of relevant subjects concerned with ethnomusicology.

1.5.3 American Studies Research Centre, Hyderabad: For the Last twenty-five years, the American Studies Research Centre at Hyderabad has been providing research resources for academics. It is a kind of academic "ashram" for college and university teachers. The Centre not only contributes to significant research in American history, literature and society, but also "encourages expanded awareness of the world and meaningful identification with all mankind".

1.6 Indian Contribution

In the total context of the present work, it is imperative to examine if India had anything to offer to the U.S. to render her already rich library and information services even richer. For obvious reasons, India could scarcely be expected to reciprocate materially even on a far more reduced scale. However, it is suggested here that the impact of Ranganathan's thought, specifically in the areas of classification and cataloguing, on scholarship in the American library world could be considered as India's intangible contribution to the U.S. Additionally, the availability of Indian librarians to work as South Asia bibliographers in some research libraries in the U.S. has helped the Library of Congress to fulfil the objectives of its PL 480 Program in an effective way.

2.7 Ever since the Second World War, cultural contacts gained recognition as an important dimension of relations between U.S. and India. The preceding pages have chronicled the library relations that emerged and were strengthened between them during the last three quarters of the century, as essentially a part, and a vital part, of that relationship.

APPENDICES

APPENDIX I

AMERICAN LIBRARY SPECIALISTS TO INDIA AS LIBRARIANS/LIBRARY DIRECTORS

Sl. No.	Name of the Specialist	Year/s of visit	Institution where worked
1	Anna G. Banker	1964-66	ACC
2.	William W. Bennett	1965	ACD
3.	W. A. Borden	1910-13	State Library, Baroda
4.	Ruth J. Caine	1951-54	ACM
5.	Dorothy L. Clark	1957-66	ACB
		1966-79,	American Studies Research Centre, Hyderabad.
6.	Thomas S. Cleveland	1960-63	Cultural Attache Officer in USIS (Place not mentioned)
7.	Richard Darlington	NA	AC (Place not mentioned)
8.	Asa Don Dickinson	1915-16	Punjab University, Lahore.
9.	Katharine S. Diehl	1961-62	Serampore College, Serampore
		1967-69	American Institute of Indian Studies, Calcutta
			University of Bombay, Bombay.
10.	Sara Margaret Dilley	1957-62	ACD
11.	Dave G. Donovan	NA	AC (Place not mentioned)
12.	Lucile Dudgeon	1944-46	ACB
13.	Anna Erickson	Early 1950s	ACD
14.	Jane Fairweather	1950-56	ACC
15.	Louis Flanagan	1970-72	ACC
16.	Martha Guse	1949-51	ACM
17.	Wayne M. Hartwell	1946-51	Cultural Attache Officer in USIS (Place not mentioned)
18.	Donald C. Hausrath	1983	ACD (Libraries and Books Services Officer)
19.	Juliane M. Heyman	1951-52	Press Secretary in USIS, Delhi
20.	Dorris A. Hunter	1950-52	ACC
21.	Cecilia Johnson	1954-61	ACM
22.	Ruth C. Krueger	1957-61	ACC
23.	Ann Donovan Lee	1987 to date	ACD (Libraries and Book Services Officer)
24.	William H. Lewis	1955-59	ACL
25.	Flora B. Ludington	1944-46	ACB
26.	Margaret F. Mackeller	1970s	ACD

(Contd.)

Appendix I *(Contd.)*

Sl. No.	Name of the Specialist	Year/s of visit	Institution where worked
27.	Evelyn McCube	1961-66	ACM
28.	Honor McCusker	1953-57	ACD
29.	Michael B. Pipkin	1980s	ACD (Libraries and Books Services Officer)
30.	Elizabeth Randles	1968-70	ACM
31.	Annadale Riley	1967-69	ACC
32.	Elizabeth G. Robb	1947-52	ACD
33.	Joseph E. Sakey	1952-53	AC (Place not mentioned)
34.	Emma K. Skinner	1954-56	ACM
35.	Dorothy E. Spofford	1966-68	ACM
36.	Elizabeth A. Winn	1951-53	ACC
37.	Mary E. Woodward	1967-70	ACB

Abbreviations used:

AC	American Center
ACB	American Center, Bombay
ACC	American Center, Calcutta
ACD	American Center, Delhi
ACL	American Center, Lucknow
ACM	American Center, Madras.

APPENDIX II

AMERICAN LIBRARY SPECIALISTS TO INDIA UNDER DIFFERENT PROGRAMMES

Sl. No.	Name of the Specialist	Year/s of visit	Institution worked in/represented
*	Lucile Dudgeon	1954-55	India Wheat Loan Educational Exchange Program
1.	Beatrice Holt	1955-61	-do-
2.	John Alden	1958	-do-
3.	Archie McNeal	1957	-do-
4.	Jennings Wood	1958-59	-do-
		1961-62	-do-
5.	Laurence J Kipp	1960-61	-do-
6.	Cecilia Rae Kipp	1960-61	-do-
7.	Horace I. Poleman	1939-40	Library of Congress Acquisitions Program
		1947	-do-
		1950-52	Cultural Attache Officer
		1961	Short term assignment
		1963-64	-do-
8.	John C. Crawford	1961	Library of Congress PL 480
		1985	Acquisitions Program
9.	Robert D. Stevens	1961	-do-
		1962	-do-
10.	John Charles Finzi	1961-64	-do-
11.	Billy Neil Sweerus	1962	-do-
12.	Eunice M. Stuzman	1962	-do-
	(Mrs. Eunice S. Gupta)	1972-74	-do-
13.	Conrad Eaton	1964-69	-do-
14.	Rodney G. Searle	1969-72	-do-
15.	Jerry R. James	1974-80	-do-
16.	E. Gene Smith	1974-77	-do-
		1980-85	-do-
17.	Michael J. Costin	1974-75	-do-
18.	Alice L. Kinskern	1976-77	-do-
19.	Helen Poe	1983	-do-

* Included in Appendix I and hence not numbered.

APPENDIX III

AMERICAN LIBRARY SPECIALISTS ASSIGNED TO INDIA SPECIALISTS AT INDIVIDUAL INSTITUTIONS

Sl. No.	Name of the Specialist	Year/s of visit	Institution worked in/represented
1.	Carl M. White	1965	University of Delhi, Delhi.
2.	Morris A. Gelfand	1966	-do-
3.	George S. Bonn	1968	-do-
4.	Carl W. Hintz	1961	University of Rajasthan, Jaipur.
5.	Jesse H. Shera	1967	Documentation Research and Training Centre, Bangalore, (IN ABSENTIA)
6.	Pauline A. Atherton	1970	DRTC, Bangalore
7.	Jean M. Perreault	1975	-do-
8.	Charles P. Bourne	1978	-do-
9.	Eugene Garfield	Sometime Information not available before 1969	
		1974	Indian Academy of Sciences, Bangalore.
		1983	DRTC, Bangalore
10.	Patrick R. Penland	1976	DRTC, Bangalore
		1985	SNDT Women's University, Bombay.
11.	Oliver C. Dunn	1962 1964 1966 1968	Indian Institute of Technology, Kanpur.
12.	George R. Meluch	1962-64	-do-
13.	Richard Funkhouser	1964-66	-do-
14.	Robert Cain	1966-67	-do-
15.	Margaret Berg	1966-67	-do-
16.	Irma Johnson	1968	-do-
*.	Dorothy L. Clark	1966-79	American Studies Research Centre, Hyderabad.
17.	John R. Russell	1966-67	-do-
18.	Margaret R. Russell	1966-67	-do-
19.	Jo Manning	1979	-do-
20.	Ronald Chapman	1985	-do-
21.	Ellen Chapman	1985	-do-
22.	Eugene deBenko	1963	College of Engineering, Guindy, Madras.

* Numbered in Appendix I.

APPENDIX IV

AMERICAN LIBRARY SPECIALISTS ASSIGNED TO INDIA AS SPECIALISTS AT AGRICULTURAL INSTITUTIONS

Sl. No.	Name of the Specialist	Year/s of visit
1.	Ralph R. Shaw	1956
2.	Dorothy M. Parker	1967
3.	Ning Yu Li	1967
4.	Angelina Carabelli	1967
5.	Don W. Jett	1968
6.	Hilary D. Burton	1983
7.	Trudy Brekelbaum	1983

APPENDIX V

AMERICAN LIBRARY SPECIALISTS ASSIGNED TO INDIA AS SPECIALISTS WITH SHORT-TERM ASSIGNMENTS

Sl. No.	Name of the Specialist	Year/s of visit
1.	Sarah K. Vann	1964
2.	Henry Scholberg	Eight times between 1964-1985
3.	James E. Agenbroad	1980; 1982

APPENDIX VI

AMERICAN LIBRARY SPECIALISTS ASSIGNED TO INDIA AS DELEGATES TO SEMINARS/CONFERENCES

Sl. No.	Name of the Specialist	Seminar/Conference attended
1.	Jay E. Daily	Unesco Seminar at Delhi, 1960
*	Pauline A. Atherton	Third International Study Conference on Classification Research held at Bombay, 1975.
2.	Harold Borko	-do-
*	Eugene Garfield	-do-
3.	David F. Hersey	-do-
4.	J. P. Immroth	-do-
*	F. W. Lancaster	-do-
5.	Christine A Montgomery	-do-
6.	Malcolm Rigby	-do-
7.	J. H. Schneider	-do-
8.	J. R. R. Dere-Mountague	-do-
9.	R. N. Paul	-do-
10.	Carole Brown Ganz	Indo-US Seminar on Scientific and Technical Information held at Bangalore, 1977.
11.	Neil Haley	-do-
12.	Mary Agnes Huffier	-do-
**	David F. Hersey	-do-
13.	Billie Griffith Barr	-do-
14.	Dorothy Elaine Caruso	-do-
15.	Donald John Hillman	-do-
16.	Vladimir Slamecka	-do-
17.	Joseph George Gratton	-do-
18.	Pranas Zunde	Third Indo-U.S. Workshop on Scientific and Technological Information held at Delhi, 1980.
19.	William Nugent	-do-
20.	Marshall C. Yovits	-do-
21.	Vernon E. Palmour	-do-
***	Donald John Hillman	-do-
22.	Michael D. Cooper	-do-
23	H. L. Resnikoff	-do-

* Included in Appendix III and hence not numbered.

** Listed at Sl. No. 3 and hence not numbered.

*** Listed at Sr. No. 15 and hence not numbered.

APPENDIX VII

AMERICAN LIBRARY SPECIALISTS ASSIGNED TO INDIA INCLUDING PERSONS FROM NON-LIBRARY WORLD

Sl. No.	Name of the Specialist	Year/s of visit
1.	Lester E. Asheim	1963; 1964
2.	Paul Bixler	1962-63
3.	Daniel J. Boorstin	1984
4.	J. Arthur Branch	1968
5.	Jack Dalton	1957; 1958; 1959
6.	Werner B. Ellinger	1960-61
7.	Luther H. Evans	1951
8.	Welthy Fisher	1939; 1947; 1952
9.	Cynthia B. Geiser	1961
10.	H. Tyler Gemmell	1966-67
11.	Richard Greenfield	1988
12.	John F. Harvey	1970
13.	Alan L. Heyneman	1955
14.	Miles M. Jackson	1983
15.	F. W. Lancaster	1980; 1985
16.	Keyes D. Metcalf	1959
17.	Raymond P. Morris	1960
18.	Quincy Mumford	1963
19.	Maureen L. P. Patterson	Number of times during 1944-82
20.	Avila A. Pelletier	1952-55
21	David T. Ray	1962-63
22.	Antoinette Strobine	1971
23.	Raynard C. Swank	1960
24.	Paul Wasserman	1981; 1987
25.	William Webb	1988
26.	Helen E. Wessells	1950
27.	Malcolm M. Willey	1968

APPENDIX VIII

INDIAN LIBRARIANS VISITING THE U.S.A. UNDER THE WHEAT LOAN EDUCATIONAL EXCHANGE PROGRAM

Sl. No.	Name	Designation	Institution
BATCH I (1955)			
1.	Nabi Ahmed	Librarian	Jamia Millia, Delhi
2.	J. C. Anand	-do-	Central Education Library, New Delhi
3.	B. C. Banerjea	Assistant Librarian	Visva-Bharati University, Santhiniketan
4.	S. Bashiruddin	Librarian	Aligarh University, Aligarh.
5.	P. C. Bose	-do-	Calcutta University, Calcutta.
6.	S. Das Gupta	-do-	Delhi University, Delhi
7.	K. R. Desai	-do-	Gujarat University, Ahmedabad
8.	B. V. Raghavendra Rao	-do-	Indian Institute of Science, Bangalore
9.	S. Ramabhadran	Assistant Librarian	Delhi University, Delhi
10.	D. C. Sarkar	Librarian	Bengal Engineering College, Sibpur
11.	A. Sharma	-do-	Delhi Polytechnic, Delhi.
12.	M. B. Vajifdar	Deputy Librarian	Tata Institute of Fundamental Research, Bombay
BATCH II (1955-56)			
1.	B. Anderson	Assistant Librarian	Bombay University, Bombay
2.	P. K. Banerjea	-do-	Agra University, Agra
3.	K. S. Deshpande	Librarian	Karnatak University, Dharwad
4.	K. S. Hingwe	-do-	Poona University, Pune
5.	J. M. Kanitkar	-do-	Indian Institute of Public Administration, New Delhi
6.	A. K. Mukherjee	Assistant Librarian	Indian Institute of Technology, Kharagpur
7.	B. L. Pathak	Librarian	Saugar University, Saugar
8.	B. Sengupta	Superintendent, Cataloguing Division	National Library, Calcutta
9.	Tara Singh	Assistant Librarian	Lucknow University, Lucknow
10.	B. K. Trivedi	-do-	Allahabad University, Allahabad
11.	Masood Yazdani	Librarian	Osmania University, Hyderabad

(Contd.)

Appendix VIII *(Contd.)*

Sl. No.	Name	Designation	Institution
BATCH III (1959)			
1.	S. S. Lal	Assistant Librarian	Punjab University, Chandigarh
2.	S. N. Mathur	-do-	Rajasthan University, Jaipur
3.	P. S. Patnaik	-do-	Sri Venkateswara University, Tirupati
4.	C. P. Shukla	Librarian	M. S. University, Baroda
BATCH IV (1960)			
1.	V. Durairajan	Assistant Librarian	Annamalai University, Chidambaram
2.	K. A. Isaac	Librarian	Kerala University, Trivandrum
3.	M. L. Kaul	Assistant Librarian	Jammu and Kashmir University, Srinagar
4.	Vidyut Khandwala	Librarian	S. N. D. T. Women's University, Bombay.
5.	B. P. Misra	-do-	Patna University, Patna

APPENDIX IX

INDIAN LIBRARIANS VISITING THE UNITED STATES FOR ADVANCED TRAINING

Sl. No.	Name	Year/s of visit
Fulbright Study Grants:		
1.	M. Mathew John	1950-52
2.	Jibananda Saha	1951-52
3.	B. K. Datta	1952-53
4.	Indu V. Nawathe	1952-53
5.	A. Neelameghan	1953-54
6.	D. S. Mehta	1954-55
7.	P. C. Randeria	1954-55
8.	H. D. Sharma	1954-55
9.	A. Krishnan	1955-56
10.	K. H. Bendigeri	1957-58
11.	R. Chakrabartibiswas	1959-60
12.	U. D. Sharma	1964-66
Fulbright Senior Research Grants:		
13.	M. L. Nagar	1951-56
14.	S. S. Saith	1952-53
15.	G. J. Narayana	1986
16.	M. A. Gopinath	1988
U.S. Foundations Including U. N. Grants:		
1.	S. Parthasarathy	1950-51
2.	D. N. Sharma	1957-59
3.	T. N. Rajan	1957-60
4.	Surinder Nath	1959-60
5.	K. D. Singh	1960
6.	P. B. Mangla	1961-62
7.	Narinder Dutta	1961-62
8.	Girija Kumar	1962
9.	N. M. Ketkar	1950

(Contd.)

Appendix IX *(Contd.)*

Sl. No.	Name	Year/s of visit
U.S. Government Including State Department, International Visitors and all U.S. Government Visits Other Than Those Under USAID or Fulbright Grants:		
1.	D. R. Kalia	1950-51 and 1966
2.	B. S. Kesavan	1954
3.	R. S. Saxena	1955
4.	Kamla Kapoor	1956
5.	K. L. Kaul	1957
6.	N. N. Mohanty	1961-62
7.	V. B. Nanda	1961-62
8.	P. N. Gour	1962-63
9.	A. P. Srivastava	1964
10.	P. S. G. Kumar	1988
Private Students including those with University Aids:		
1.	Mukti Kapila	1952-53
2.	H. C. Pandey	1956
3.	Heera Kapasi	1958-59
4.	R. K. Mehrotra	1960-61
5.	A. A. G. Khan	1961-63
6.	S. K. Lakhanpal	1961-66
7.	A. L. Kapoor	1964-65
USAID Grants:		
1.	M. K. Kelkar	1965-66
Government of India Grants:		
1.	O. S. Sachdeva	1959-60
Private including Tourists, Business and Professional Men:		
1.	S. L. Sawhney	1964

BIBLIOGRAPHY

BOOKS

Alden, John. *Report to Mr. B. S. Kesavan, Librarian, National Library, Calcutta. 8 May 1958*. Typescript.

Amatsuchi, Haruki, *et al. American Libraries: Report of the U.S. Field Seminar on Library Reference Services for Japanese Librarians*. Tokyo, International House of Japan, Inc., 1960. pp. 147.

American Institute of Indian Studies. *American Institute of Indian Studies: A pamphlet*.

Anderson, Florence. *Carnegie Corporation Library Program, 1911-1961*. New York, Carnegie Corporation of New York, 1963. p. 101.

Applebaum, Edmond L. "Foreign acquisitions programs of the Library of Congress." In *Acquisitions of Foreign Materials for U.S. Libraries* edited by Theodore Samore. Metuchen (N. J.). The Scarecrow Press, Inc., 1982. pp. 15-25.

Asheim, Lester. *Librarianship in the Developing Countries*. Urbana, University of Illinois Press, 1966. p. 95.

—, "Sponsored tours for foreign librarians in the United States." in *Library Education and Training in Developing Countries* edited by George S Bonn. Honolulu, East-West Center Press, 1967. pp. 38-44.

"The Asia Foundation. "in *The Bowker Annual of Library and Book Trade Information*. New York, R. R. Bowker Company, 1978. pp. 405-06.

Atherton, Pauline A. *Putting Knowledge to Work: An American View of Ranganathan's Five Laws of Library Science*. Delhi, Vikas Publishing House Pvt. Ltd., 1973. p. 158.

Badri Narain. *The Impact of the Wheat Loan Assistance given by the U.S. A. for the Development of Libraries and Librarians in India–A term paper* (project report). Chandigarh, Punjab University, 1962. p. 59.

Ball, Alice Dulany. "Universal Serials and Book Exchange, Inc." in *Encyclopedia of Library and Information Science*, Vol. 32, edited by Allen Kent and others. New York, Marcel Dekker Inc., 1981. pp. 146-51.

Barnett, Stanley A. and Piggford Roland R. *Manual on Book and Library Activities in Developing Countries*. Washington (D. C.), Agency for International Development, 1969. p 235.

Barrier, N. Gerald, *India and America: American Publishing on India, 1930-1985*, New Delhi, Manohar Publications, 1986, p. 333

Benjamin, Curtis G. *U.S. Books Abroad: Neglected Ambassadors*. Washington (D. C.), Library of Congress, 1984. p. 95.

Bhandarkar, S. S. *The Story of Pantnagar: A Short History of the G. B. Pant University of Agriculture and Technology, Pantnagar, 1960-1975*. Manuscript. 1975.

Bhattacharyya, Ganesh. "Relevance of Ranganathan's ideas in the context of modern development." in *New Trends in International Librarianship: S. R. Ranganathan festschrift to mark the Platinum Jubilee of the Madras University Library*. edited by P. A. Mohanrajan. New Delhi, Allied Publication Pvt. Ltd., 1984. pp. 226-33.

Bourne, Charles P. *Technology in Support of Library Science and Information Service with Particular Emphasis on Computer-assisted Reference Service*. Bangalore, Sarada Ranganathan Endowment for Library Science, 1980. p. 78.

Brewster, Beverly J. *American Overseas Library Technical Assistance, 1940-1970*. Metuchen (N. J.), the Scarecrow Press, Inc., 1976. p. 434.

Busha, C. H. and Harter, S. P. *Research Methods in Librarianship Techniques and Interpretations*. New York, The Academic Press, 1980. p. 417.

Chagla, M. C. "Our common heritage." in *American Studies in India: Proceedings of the Inauguration of the American Studies Research Centre at Osmania University, Hyderabad, 4 April 1964*. New Delhi, The United States Information Service, 1964. p. 6-9.

Chandran, D. *An Assessment of the Development of Madurai University Library*. A project report submitted to the University of Mysore as a partial fulfilment for the Master's Degreee in Library Science. Mysore, University of Mysore, 1974.

Conant, Ralph W. *The Conant Report: A Study of the Education of Librarians*. Cambridge, The Massachusetts Institute of Technology Press, 1980. p. 210.

Dagli, Vadilal. (Ed.) *Two Decades of Indo-U.S. Relations*. Bombay, Vora & Co. Publishers Pvt. Ltd., 1969. p. 231.

Danton, J. Periam. *Book Selection and Collections: A Comparison of German and American University Libraries*. New York, Columbia University Press, 1963. p. 188.

—, "Definitions of comparative and international library science." in *Comparative and International Library Science*. edited by John F. Harvey. Metuchen (N. J.). The Scarecrow Press, Inc. 1977. pp. 3-14.

—, *United States Influence on Norwegian Librarianship, 1890-1940*. Los Angeles, University of California Press, 1957. p. 91.

Deshmukh, C. D. *The Course of My Life*. New Delhi, Orient Longman Ltd., 1974. p. 367.

Deshpande, K. S., *Land of Libraries: Story of a Study Tour of the U.S.A.*, Hubli, The Gurudeva Literary Association, 1958, p. 84.

Dickinson, Asa Don. *Panjab Library Primer*. Lahore, University of the Panjab, 1916. p. 242.

Dix, William S. "The Public Law 480 Program and the National Program for Acquisition and Cataloging of the Library of Congress." in *Acquisitions from the Third World-papers of the Ligue des Bibliotheques Europeennes de Recherche seminar 17-19 September 1973*. edited by D. A. Clarke. London, Mansell Information Publishing Limited, 1975. pp. 159-76.

Embassy of the United States of America, New Delhi, *Indo-U.S. Cooperation in Education and Culture*, New Delhi, Embassy of the United States of America, p. 48.

Fisher, Glen. *American Communication in a Global Society*. Norwood (N. J.), Ablex Publishing Corporation, 1979. p. 165.

Fisher, Welthy. *Literacy and Development: A Commemorative Volume for Welthy Honsinger Fisher*. Delhi, the Dr. Welthy Fisher farewell reception committee in India, 1973. p. 38.

Ford Foundation. *The Ford Foundation and Foundation Supported Activities in India*. New Delhi, Ford Foundation. 1955. p. 106.

—. *The Ford Foundation and Foundation Supported Activities in India: Summary of Grants from 1951 to 1969*. New Delhi, Ford Foundation. p. 33.

Fosdick, Raymond B. The Story of the Rockefeller Foundation. New York, Harper and Brothers, 1982. p. 336.

Foskett, D. J. "Ranganathan's professionalism." in *S. R. Raganathan, 1892-1972* edited by Edward Dudley. London, The Library Association, 1974. p. 23-25.

Garfield, Eugene. "A tribute to S. R. Ranganathan." in *New Trends in International Librarianship: S. R. Ranganathan Festschrift to mark the Platinum Jubilee of the Madras University Library.* edited by P A. Mohanrajan. New Delhi, Allied Publishers Pvt., Ltd., 1984. pp. 263-79.

Gelfand, Morris A. *Survey of University of Delhi Department of Library Science*. mimeographed. 1966.

Girja Kumar. "South Asian traditional studies and modern area studies: Their impact on libraries." in *International Cooperation in Orientalist Librarianship: Papers Presented at the Library Seminars, 28th International Congress* of Orientalists, Canberra, 6-12 January 1971 edited by Enid Bishop and Jean M. Waller. Canberra, National Library of Australia, 1972, pp. 251-62.

Gitler, Robert L. "Library education–the global scene." in *Library Education and Training in Developing Countries* edited by George S. Bonn. Honolulu, East West Center Press, 1967. pp. 5-26.

Gnanamuttu, S. "Madurai University Library–A decade of progress." in *Madurai University Library 10th Anniversary Souvenir*. Madurai, Madurai University, 1968. pp. 1-5.

Goodwin, Craufurd D. "International dimensions: The international involvement of American Libraries." in *Libraries at Large: Tradition, Innovation and the National Interest* edited by D. M. Knight and E. S. Nourse. New York, R. R. Bowker Company, 1969. pp. 559-89.

Hausrath, Donald C. "United States Information Agency book and library programs." in *The Bowker Annual of Library and Book Trade Information*. New York, R. R. Bowker Company, 1985. pp. 130-40.

Hewitt, Vivian D. "Services to library life abroad. " in *A century of Service: Librarianship in the United States* and *Canada* edited by Sidney L. Jackson *et al*. Chicago, American Library Association, 1976. pp. 321-40.

Hintz, Carl W. *Education for Librarianship in India*. Urbana, University of Illinois, 1964. mimeographed.

Hungund, B. B. *Development of University Libraries in India*. M. Lib. Sc. Dissertation. Bombay University. 1969.

Inamdar, N. B. and Riswadkar, M. R. "India." in *International Handbook of Contemporary Developments in Librarianship* edited by Miles M. Jackson. Westport (Connecticut), Greenwood Press, 1981. pp. 183-99.

India: A Statistical Outline. New Delhi, Oxford & IBH Publishing Co., 1984. p. 210.

India Government. *Report on the Indo-U.S. Technological Cooperation Programme*. New Delhi, India Government (Ministry of Finance) 1961. p. 194.

India Government (Department of Science and Technology). *Third Indo-U.S. Workshop on Scientific and Technological Information, 10-12 March 1980: Workshop Proceedings*. New Delhi, Government of India. 1980. p. 157.

India 1984: A Reference Annual. New Delhi, Government of India, 1985.

India Wheat Loan Educational Exchange Program–A Pamphlet. New Delhi, United States Information Service, 1955. p. 11.

Jay, Donald F. Paper presented at the conference on *The Impact of the Public Law 480 Program on Overseas Acquisitions by American Libraries*, held at the Wisconsin Center, Madison, Wisconsin, 12 May 1967. Mimeographed.

Jett, Don W. *Mysore University of Agricultural Sciences: Library Development Consultant Report*. 1968, Mimeographed.

Johnson, Elmer D. and Harris, Michael H. *History of Libraries in the Western World*. Metuchen (N. J.) the Scarecrow Press. Inc., 1976. p. 354.

Kalia, D. R. and Mehta J. C. "The impact of recent developments on Indian libraries." in *International Librarianship* edited by George Chandler. London, Library Association, 1972. pp. 49-53.

Kamath, M. V. *The United States and India 1776-1976*. Washington (D. C.), The Embassy of India, 1976. p. 222.

Kamen, Susan Van. "Programs in support of international studies at the Center for Research Libraries." in *Acquisition of Foreign Materials for U.S. Libraries* edited by Theodore Samore. Metuchen (N. J.), The Scarecrow Press, Inc. 1982. pp. 176-85.

Kapasi, Heera. "USIS Libraries in India with special reference to the American Center Library, New Delhi." in *Handbook of Libraries, Archives and Information Centres in India*, Vol. 1. edited by B. M.

Gupta *et al.* New Delhi, Information Industry Publication, 1984-85. pp. 181-87.

Kayastha, Ved P. "Development of Indian and other South Asian Collections in the United States." in *Indian Librarianship–Perspectives and prospects* edited by Ravindra Nath Sharma. New Delhi, Kalyani Publishers, 1981. pp. 286-307.

Kelly, Colleen Adele. *The Educational Philosophy and Work of Welthy Honsinger Fisher in China and India*, 1906-1980. Ph. D. Dissertation. University of Connecticut. 1983.

Kemp, D. A. "American librarianship–A British view." in *Library Literature 10: The best of 1979*. edited by Bill Katz. Metuchen (N. J.), The Scarecrow Press, Inc. 1980. pp. 120-34.

Kesavan, B. S. *India's National Library*. Calcutta, National Library, 1961. p. 300.

Khandwala. Vidyut K. "My experience of an American university library." in *Development of Libraries in New India* edited by N. B. Sen. New Delhi, New Book Society of India, 1965. pp. 227-33.

Kipp, Laurence J. and Kipp, Cecilia Rae. *Indian Libraries and the India Wheat Loan Educational Exchange Program: A Report*. Mimeographed. 1961.

Kraske, Gary E., *Missionaries of the Book: The American Library Profession and the Origins of United States Cultural Diplomacy*, Westport (Connecticut), Greenwood Press, 1985, pp. 293.

Krishan Kumar and Sardana, J. L. "Research in library and information science." in *Library and Information Science Education in India: Papers and Recommendations of an All India Seminar held at the Department of Library Science*, University of Delhi, during 3-8 October, 1977 edited by P. B. Mangla. Delhi, Macmillan India Limited, 1981. pp. 121-45.

Krzys, Richard. International and comparative study in librarianship: Research methodology." in *Encyclopedia of Library and Information Science*, Vol 12, edited by Allen Kent *et al.* New York, Marcel Dekker Inc., 1974. pp. 325-43.

Krzys, Richard and Litton, Gaston. *World Librarianship: A Comparative Study*. New York, Marcel Dekker Inc. 1983. pp. 239

Kudalkar. J. S. *The Baroda Library Movement: A Short Account of the Origin and Growth of the Central Library Department of the Baroda State*. Baroda. Baroda Central Library, 1919. p. 78.

Kumar, P. S. G. *Profiles of American Libraries*, New Delhi, Indus Publishing Company, 1989, pp. 230.

Lancaster, F. W. "The library as a growing organism." in *Ranganathan's Philosophy: Assessment, Impact and Relevance: Proceedings of the International Conference organised by Indian Library Association and co-sponsored by Sarada Ranganathan Endowment for Library Science*. edited by T. S. Rajagopalan. New Delhi, Vikas Publishing House Pvt. Ltd., 1986. pp. 51-53

Lancaster, F. W. and Mehrotra, Rashmi. "Five Laws of Library Science as a guide to the evaluation of library services." in *Perspectives in Library and Information Science (Viswanathan festschrift)*, Vol. 1, edited by S. N. Agarwal *et al.*, Lucknow, Print House (India), 1982. pp. 26-39.

Liebaers, Herman. "The impact of American and European librarianship upon each other". in *Libraries and the Life of the Mind in America: Addresses Delivered at the Centennial Celebration of the American Library Association.* Chicago, American Library Association, 1977. pp. 65-83.

Ludington, Flora B. *Report on India.* 1946. Manuscript.

McMurry, Ruth Emily and Lee, Muna. *The Cultural Approach: Another Way in International Relations.* Chapel Hill, The University of North Carolina Press, 1947. p. 280.

Magat, Richard. *The Ford Foundation at Work: Philanthropic Choices Methods and Styles.* New York, Plenum Press, 1979. p. 207.

Malik, Harji. *America's Unique Libraries.* Mimeographed.

Mangla, P. B. "Research in library and information science in U.S.A., U.K. and India: An overview." in *Perspectives in Library and Information Science (Viswanathan Festschrift)*, Vol. 2 edited by S. N. Agarwal *et al.*, Lucknow, Print House (India), 1982. pp. 44-61.

Marshall, D.N. *History of Libraries–Ancient and Mediaeval.* New Delhi, Oxford and IBH publishing Co., 1983. p. 151.

Mathews, Geraldine O. *The Influence of Ranganathan on Faceted Classification.* Ph. D. Dissertation. Case Western Reserve University. 1980.

Myer, Robert A. "Ford Foundation." in *Encyclopedia of Library and Information Science*, Vol. 8, edited by Allen Kent and Harold Lancour. New York, Marcel Dekker, Inc., 1972. pp. 592-600.

Mehrotra, R. K. and Joginder Singh. "American Centre Library, New Delhi: Its services and resources." in *Perspectives in Library and Information Science (Viswanathan festschrift)* Vol. 1, edited by S. N. Agarwal *et al.* Lucknow, Print House (India), 1982. pp. 124-28.

Mukherjee, A. K, *Librarianship: Its Philosophy and History*. Bombay, Asia Publishing House, 1966. p. 220.

Munthe, Wilhelm, *American Librarianship from a European Angle: An Attempt at an Evaluation of Policies and Activities*. Chicago, American Library Association, 1939. p. 191.

Nagar, Murari Lal. *Public Library Movement in Baroda 1901-1949*. A Doctoral Dissertation submitted to Columbia University. 1969.

Nayak, K. C. and Sankaram, A. *A History of Agricultural Universities*. New Delhi, Oxford & IBH Publishing Co., 1972. p. 296.

Neelameghan, A. "Education for librarians and documentalists in India". in *Encyclopedia of Library and Information Science*. Vol. 11, edited by Allen Kent *et al.* New York, Marcel Dekker Inc., 1974. pp. 312-49.

—, (Ed) *Ordering Systems for Global Information Networks*: Proceedings of the Third International Study Conference on Classification Research held at Bombay, India, During 6-11 January 1975. Bangalore, Sarada Ranganathan Endowment for Library Science, 1979. p. 511.

—. "Perface" to the Sarada Ranganathan Lecture Series in Jean M. Perreault's *The Idea of Order in Bibliography*. Bangalore, Sarada Ranganathan Endowment for Library Science, 1978. p. vii.

Nisbet, Robert A. "Co-operation." in *International Encyclopedia of the Social Sciences*. Vol. 3. edited by David L. Sills. New York, The Macmillan Company and the Free Press, 1968. pp. 384-90.

Palmer, N. D. *United States and India: Dimensions of Influence*. New York, Praeger, 1984. p. 302.

Parker, Dorothy *et al. Final Report on the ICAR Institutes and Agricultural University Libraries*. New Delhi, Indian Council of Agricultural Research, 1969. p. 182.

Patterson, Maureen L. P. Paper presented at the Conference on *The Impact of the Public Law 480 Program on Overseas Acquisitions by American Libraries* held at Wisconsin Center, Madison, Wisconsin, 12 May 1967. Mimeographed.

— "South Asia library development." in *South Asian Library Resources in North America*. Papers from the Boston Conference, 1974.

Perreault, Jean M. *The Idea of Order in Bibliography*. Bangalore, Sarada Ranganathan Endowment for Library Science. 1978. pp. 135.

Phillips, Janet C., Ed. *Foreign Service Directory of American Librarians*. Pittsburgh, University of Pittsburgh Book Center, 1967. pp. 109.

Predeek, Albert. *A History of Libraries in Great Britain and North America*. Translated by Lawrence S. Thompson. Chicago, American Library Association, 1947. p. 177.

Price, Paxton P. Ed. *International Book and Library Activities: The History of a U.S. Foreign Policy*. Metuchen (N. J.), The Scarecrow Press, Inc., 1982. p. 248

Ranganathan, S. R. *Heading and Canons: Comparative Study of Five Catalogue Codes*. Madras, S. Viswanathan, 1955. p. 219.

—. *Library Tour* 1948 *Europe and America: Impressions and Reflections*. Delhi, Indian Library Association, 1950. p. 219.

—. *Prolegomena to Library Classification*. London, The Library Association, 1957. p. 487.

Rockefeller Foundation. *The Rockefeller Foundation Directory of Fellowship Awards for the years 1917-1950*. New York, Rockefeller Foundation. Year of Publication not mentioned.

Rosenthal, Joseph. *Statement on behalf of the Association of Research Libraries before the Subcommittee on Legislative Branch Appropriations. U.S. House of Representatives on Library of Congress Appropriations for fiscal year 1986*. 5 March, 1985. Typescript.

Rosinger, Lawrence K. *India and the United States: Political and Economic Relations*. New York, Macmillan Co., 1950. p. 149.

Schell, Hal B. "Library consultants and consulting." in *Encyclopedia of Library and Information Science*, Vol. 15. edited by Allen Kent *et al*. New York, Dekker, 1975. pp. 201-14.

Sharma, J. S. *The Substance of Library Science*. Bombay, Asia Publishing House, 1965. p. 244.

Sharp, Henry A. *Libraries and Librarianship in America: A British Commentary and Comparison*. London, Grafton & Co., 1936. pp. 191.

Shaw, Ralph R. and Krishna Rao, D. B. *Report on Library and Bibliographical Services for Agricultural Teaching and Research in India*. New Delhi, Indian Council of Agricultural Research, 1957. p. 59.

Shera, Jesse H. "Of peacocks, elephants and the philosophy of librarianship," in *March of Library Science (Kaula Festschrift)* edited by V. Venkatappaiah. New Delhi Vikas Publishing House Pvt. Ltd., 1979. pp. 19-25.

—. Sociological Foundations of Librarianship. Bombay, Asia Publishing House, 1970. p. 195.

—. and Perry, James W. "Changing concepts of classification: Philosophical and educational implications." in *Library Science Today. (Ranganathan festschrift)*. Vol. 1. edited by P. N. Kaula. Bombay, Asia Publishing House, 1965. pp. 37-48.

Statistical Abstract of the United States, 1985. Washington (D. C.), U.S. Bureau of the census, 1984. p. 991.

The World in figures. London, *The Economist*, 1981. p. 294

USIS, New Delhi. *Indo-American Technical Co-operation, 1952-56*. New Delhi, USIS. Year of publication not mentioned.

Vickery, B. C. "Ranganathan's contribution to indexing." in *S. R. Ranganathan. 1892-1972* edited by Edward Dudly. London, The Library Association, 1974. pp. 9-11.

White, Carl M. *A Survey of the University of Delhi Library*. Delhi, University of Delhi, 1965, p. 184.

Willey, Malcolm M. and Branch, J. Arthur. *A Self Study Manual for Indian Universities and Colleges*. Published by the Representative of the Ford Foundation in India, 1968. p. 79.

William, Gordon. Paper presented at the Conference on *The Impact of the Public Law 480 Program on Overseas Acquisitions by American Libraries*, held at the Wisconsin Center, Madison, Wisconsin. 12 May 1967. Mimeographed.

Williams, Edwin E. and Noble, Ruth V. Preliminary memoranda to the Conference on *International Cultural, Educational and Scientific Exchanges. Princeton University, November 25-26, 1946*. Chicago, American Library Association, 1947. pp. 134-43.

Williamson, Charles C. *The Williamson Reports of 1921 and 1923: Training for Library Work (1921) and Training for Library Service (1923)*. Metuchen (N. J.), The Scarecrow Press, 1971. pp. 276, pp. 165.

JOURNALS

Agrawal, Jagan Nath. "Libraries in ancient India." *Indian Librarian*. 8 (1953-54): 141-44.

Agrawal, S.S. "Ranganathan's influence on Anglo-American Cataloguing Rules." *Herald of Library Science*.

American Institute of Indian Studies. *Samvadi: ARCE Newsletter*. 1 (September 1984).

American Studies Research Centre, Hyderabad. *Newsletter*. No. 11 (December 1967): 19-20.

—. *The Month at ASRC*. March 1979.

—. *The Month* at ASRC. July 1979.

Amin, Motibhai M. "The library movement in Charotar Mitra Mandal libraries–The first library movement". *Modern Librarian*. 7 (1936-37): 30-38.

Amritjit Singh. "An experiment in academic ashram: A close range view of the American Studies Research Centre in Hyderabad, India." *International Educational and Cultural Exchange*. 20 (1977): 2-7.

Asheim, Lester. "International values in American librarianship". *Journal of Library History*. 20 (1985): 186-95.

Atherton, Pauline A. "Dr. S. R. Ranganathan." *Library Resources and Technical Services*. 14 (1970): 582-84.

—. Review of "Colon Classification." *Library Journal*. 91 (1966): 1866-68.

Awards and Citations, ALA, 1970." *Library Journal*. 95 (1970): 2636-37.

Axford, H. William. "Library education at the University of the Punjab: American influences." *Journal of Education for Librarianship*. 6 (1966): 280-89.

Banerjea, P. K. "American libraries as viewed by an Indian librarian." *Indian Librarian*. 12 (1957-58): 59-64.

Bashiruddin, S. "University libraries since independence." *Cultural Forum*. 9 (1966-67): 39-44.

Bendigeri, K. H. "Library movement in U.S.A." *Timeless Fellowship*. 9 (1974-75): 1-11.

Berninghausen, David K. "The American library consultant overseas." *International Library Review*. 1 (1969): 97-105.

Bhatia, Sant Ram. "History of libraries and the library movement in the Punjab." *Modern Librarian*. 6 (1935-36): 87-97.

—. "Training for librarianship." *Modern Librarian*. 4 (1933-34): 109-13.

Blunt, Robert. "The work of the Asia Foundation." *Pacific Affairs*. 29 (1956): 46-56.

Bonn, George S. "The state of library education in India." *Annals of Library Science and Documentation*. 15 (1968).

Borden, W. A. "Baroda, India, and its libraries." *Library Journal*. 38 (1913): 659-63.

Bose, P. C. "Training for librarianship in India." *Journal of the Indian Library Association*. 1 (1956): 30-34.

Bryant, Douglas W. "Mid-century American librarianship: Examination and experimentation." *Libri*. 7 (1958): 233-32.

Burgess, Robert S. "Education for librarianship–U.S. assistance." *Library Trends*. 20 (1971-72): 515-26.

Burke, Redmond A. "German librarianship from an American angle." *Library Quarterly*. 22 (1952): 180-93.

Byrd, Cecil K. "Introduction." *Library Trends*. 20 (1971-72): 475-77.

Carnovsky, Leon. Review of "Library Science today" edited by P. N. Kaula. *Library Quarterly*. 35 (1965): 388.

Chakravarty, N. C. "Lest we forget–pioneers who are no more." *I. L. A. Bulletin*. 3 (1967): 96-103.

—. "Librarianship in India." *I. L. A. Bulletin*. 4 (1968): 37-46.

Chakravorti, S. N. "Libraries in ancient times with special reference to India." *Indian Librarian*. 9 (1954-55): 49-57.

Chandran, D. "Madurai University Library–Progress in ten years." *I. L. A. Bulletin*. 12 (1976): 193-97.

Clapp, Verner W. "Fulbright Grants." *Library Journal*. 77 (1952): 1357-61.

Collett John. American libraries abroad: United States Information Agency activities". *Library Trends*. 20 (1972): 538-47.

Colson, John Calvin. "The writing of American library history, 1876-1976." *Library Trends*. 25 (1976-77): 7-21.

Custer, Benjamin A. Review of "Classification research" edited by Pauline Atherton. *College and Research Libraries*. 27 (1966): 492.

Das Gupta, Chidananda. "Scholarly pursuits in India–American Institute of Indian Studies." *Span*. 26 (August: 1983) 12-14.

Das Gupta, S. "A brief report on the visit to the United States of America under the India Wheat Loan Educational Exchange Programme." *Journal of the Indian Library Association*. 2 (1956-57): 27-47.

Deshpande, K. S. "The Wheat Loan Programme and its impact on the Indian library world." *Granthapal*. 4 (1961-62): 118-25.

Diehl, Katharine S. "Books and common education in the Indo-Pak sub-continent 1959-1962." *Journal of Library History*. 2 (1967): 201-10.

Diwakar, S. "Memorial to a young lady's efforts." *American Reporter*. 23 (10 January 1973): 8.

Drieberg, T. "The man with the tin trunk." *Indian Journal of Adult Education*. 40 (September 1979): 41-43.

Dudley, Norman. "The blanket order." *Library Trends*. 18 (1969-70): 318-27.

Dutt, Newton Mohun. "History of Indian libraries from earliest times to the present day." *Modern Librarian*. 2 (1931-32): 69-76.

Girja Kumar. "University libraries in India–A case study. A survey of the University of Delhi Library, Carl M. White, Planning Unit, University of Delhi." *University News*. 4 (October 1966): 17-18.

Gjelsness, Rudolph. Review of "A survey of the University of Delhi Library by Carl M. White." *College and Research Libraries*. 27 (1966): 490-91.

—. Review of "Colon Classification" 3rd ed. 1950. *Library Journal*. 76 (1951): 1798-99.

Glazier, Kenneth M. "United States influence on Canadian Universities and their libraries." *College and Research Libraries*. 28 (1967): 311-16.

Goil, N. K. "Survey of the University of Delhi Library by Carl M. White–A review." *Library Herald*. 8 (1965-66): 290-92.

Gorman, Michael. "Let us now praise–A reflective look at six persons who greatly influenced the art of cataloguing." *American Libraries*. 11 (1980): 201-03.

Greenaway, Emerson. "Progress in international librarianship. *American Libraries*. 3 (1972): 803-06.

Gupta, R. K. "A few more comments on Morris A. Gelfand's survey of Delhi Library School." *I. L. A. Bulletin*. 4 (1968): 70-72.

Guru Dutt, K. "The inwardness of Dr. Ranganathan". *Herald of Library Science*. 12 (1973).

Hansen, Agnes C. "Gold in the foreign service roaster." *A. L. A. Bulletin*. 39 (1945): 15-17.

Harris, Michael H. "Portrait in Paradox: Commitment and ambivalence in American librarianship, 1876-1976." *Libri*. 26 (1976): 281-301.

Harrison K. C. "International relations in librarianship". *I. L. A. Bulletin*. 10 (1974): 1-6.

Harvey, John F. "Kuwait city libraries." *Indian Librarian*. 28 (1973-74): 185-96.

—. "Libraries in Bombay." *Indian Librarian*. 28 (1973-74): 129-36.

——. "Libraries in Hyderabad." *Herald of Library Science*. 13 (1974): 125-35.

Harwell, Richard. "Personnel: Jack Dalton." *College and Research Libraries*. 20 (1959): 394.

Havard-Williams, P. "International librarianship". *Unesco Bulletin for Libraries*. 26 (1972): 63-68.

Herald of Library Science. "Notes and News". 2 (1963): 265: 3 (1964): 78; 10 (1971): 188 and 24 (1985): 121.

Heyman, Juliane M. "Asia Foundation libraries." *Library Journal*. 82 (1957): 2890-92.

The Hindustan Times–Evening News. 4 June 1983.

Horrocks, Norman. "The U.S. in world librarianship." *Library Journal*. 10 (1976): 221-23.

Hulbert, James A. "U.S.I.S. Library: Paris." *Library Journal*. 78 (1953): 945-48.

IASLIC Newsletter. April 1985, p. 2.

Indian Librarian. "Notes and News". 7 (1952-53): 131-32; 10 (1955-56): 126; 14.(1959-60): 201-02 and 15 (1960-61): 83.

Jackson, Miles M. "Library development abroad." *Library Journal*. 91 (1966): 1354-61.

Jain, H. C. "Achievements of academic libraries in India–a decennial review." *Library Herald*. 6 (1963-64): 172-80

Kapoor, Kamla. "The American Library: 25 years of service." *Span*. 12 (October 1971): 42-44.

Kesavan, B. S. "Carl White Report (Editorial)." *Annals of Library Science and Documentation*. 12 (1965): 119-28.

——. "Editorial." *Annals of Library Science and Documentation*. 15 (1968): 53-55.

Khurshid, Anis. "Growth of libraries in India." *International Library Review*. 4 (1972): 21-65.

——. "Library education in South Asia." *Libri*. 20 (1970): 59-76.

Kildal, Arne. "American influence on European librarianship." *Library Quarterly*. 7 (1937): 196-220.

Kuhn, Ferdinand. "Windows of the U.S." *Library Journal*. 78 (1953): 1184-87.

Labhu Ram. "Principal Woolner's dream or the phenomenal growth of the Punjab University Library." *Modern Librarian*. 4 (1933-34): 41-53.

Lal, S. S. "Punjab University extension library, Ludhiana on the march." *Indian Librarian*. 22 (1967-68): 138-42.

Library of Congress Information Bulletin. "Staff news." *LC Information Bulletin.* 43 (11): 12 March, 1984.

—. 44 (1985): 57-58.

Library Quarterly. "The contributors to the issue." 42 (1972): 345.

Library Trends. Special issue on the influence of American librarianship abroad. 20 (1971-72): 475-591.

Liebaers, Herman. "Books, libraries, librarians: European and American style. " *Journal of Library History.* 8 (1973): 18-22.

Lohrer, Alice and Jackson, William V. "Education and training of librarians in Asia, the Near East and Latin America." *Library Trends.* 8 (1959-60): 243-77.

Ludington, Flora B. "The American contribution to foreign library establishment and rehabilitation." *Library Quarterly.* 24 (1954): 192-204.

McNeal, Archie L. "Academic and research libraries in India." *College and Research Libraries.* 20 (1959): 243-46.

Mangla, P. B. "Survey of University of Delhi, Department of Library Science (1966) by Morris A. Gelfand–An evaluation. " *I. L. A. Bulletin.* 3 (1967): 137-47.

Mangla, P.B. and Vashishth, C. P. Library and information science education in India." *Journal of Library and Information Science.* 1 (1976): 127-60.

Merrill, William S. Review of "Colon Classification (1933)." *Library Journal.* 58 (1933): 782-83.

Modern Librarian. "The library movement in the Punjab–Paper submitted by the Library Association, Lahore, to the All-Asia Educational Conference held at Benares on December 26-30, 1930." *Modern Librarian.* 1 (1930-31): 55-58.

Mohinder Singh. "Progress in librarianship in India 1911-1978." *Libri* 29 (1979): 158-68.

Moon, Eric. "Editorial." *Library Journal.* 85 (15 November 1960): 4114.

Mosteller, John, University of Pennsylvania Indian Art and Architecture Photographic Archival Collection. A paper presented at the Meeting of the Association for Asian Studies, Mid Atlantic Region at Drew University, Madison (N. J.), on October 24-26, 1980. Typescript.

Mukherjee, A. K. "Wheat Loan Educational Exchange Programme in India and the Indian university libraries." *Library Herald.* 6 (1963-64): 96-102.

Nagar, Murari Lal, Ed. Wheat Loan Messenger–Report of the Proceedings of the fifth Wheat Loan library workshop, Delhi, March 5-9, 1962. No. 3 (January 1963): 116.

O'Loughlin, M. Anne John. *The Emergence of American Librarianship: A Study of Influences Evident in 1876*. D. L. S. Dissertation. Columbia University, 1971: 269.

Parker, J. Stephen. "International librarianship–a reconnaissance." *Journal of Librarianship*. 6 (1974): 219-32.

—. "The overseas library consultant." *Library Review*. 28 (1979): 214-25.

Patterson, Maureen L. P. "South Asian area studies and the library". *Library Quarterly*. 35 (1965): 223-34.

—. "The South Asian PL 480 Library Program, 1962-1968." *Journal of Asian Studies*. 28 (1969): 743-54.

Perreault, Jean M. Review of "Colon Classification." *Library Resources and Technical Services*. 11 (1967): 121-22.

Qureshi, Naimuddin. "Comparative and international Librarianship: An analytical approach." *Unesco Journal of Information Science, Librarianship and Archives Administration*. 2 (1980): 22-28.

Ramakrishna Rao. K. "Library development in India." *Library Quarterly*. 31 (1961): 135-53.

Ranganathan, S. R. "Asia's contribution to library classification." *Ceylon Library Review*. 4 (1971): 11-24.

—. "Library personality of India". *Library Journal*. 76 (1951): 155-57.

—. "Library science and scientific method." *Annals of Library Science*. 4 (1957): 19-32.

—. "Pre-Natal Classification and Cataloguing on its way." *Annals of Library Science*. 6 (1959): 113-25.

Rayward, W. Boyd. "Librarianship in the New World and the Old: Some points of contact." *Library Trends*. 25 (1976-77): 209-26.

Reith, David. "Indo-American co-operation in librarianship." *International Library Review*. 14 (1982): 263-81.

Reparata, Mary. Review of "Colon Classification (1933)" *Library Quarterly*. 4 (1934): 501-04.

Reynolds, Michael M. "Library Co-operation: The ideal and the reality." *College and Research Libraries*. 35 (1974): 424-31.

Richmond, Phyllis A. Review of "Colon Classification." 6th ed. 1960. *Library Quarterly*. 32 (1962): 99-100.

Rovelstad, Mathilde V. "A new international librarianship: A challenge to the profession." *Unesco Bulletin for Libraries*. 32 (1978): 136-43 and 153.

Ryan, Frederick. "Librarianship Soviet style." *Library Journal*. 106 (1981): 2360-64.

Sahi, Manu. "American Libraries in India." *Span*. 22 (March 1981): 10-13.

Samore, Theodore. "Acquisition of materials from third world countries for U.S. libraries." *Library Acquisitions: Practice and Theory*. 6 (1982): 107-12.

Sengupta, B. "Libraries and library movement in India." *Indian Librarian*. 15 (1960-61): 9-15.

Sharma, C. D. "From other continents: A study of British and American libraries in India." *Lucknow Librarian*. 3 (1964): 65-81.

Sharma, Dev Raj. "Doctoral degrees awarded by Indian universities during 1957-1984 in library and information science." *CLIS Observer*. 2 (1985): 18-23.

Sharma, O. P. "The development of library education in India: an historical survey." *Library Association Reccrd*. 67 (1965): 388-94.

Sharma, Ravindra Nath. "Asian sources in American libraries." *Libri*. 34 (1984): 27-43.

Shastri, Raghunandan. "Book-activity in ancient India." *Indian Librarian*. 6 (1951-52): 16-18.

Shepard, M. D. "International dimensions of U.S. librarianship." *A. L. A. Bulletin*. 62 (1968): 699-710.

Shera, Jesse H. "Failure and success: Assessing a century." *Library Journal*. 101 (1976): 281-87.

—. "The literature of American library history." *Library Quarterly*. 15 (1945): 1-24.

—. Review of "Colon Classification." 3rd ed. 1950. *Library Quarterly*. 22 (1952): 59-61.

—. Review of S. R. Ranganathan's Library book selection" and other books. *Library Quarterly*. 24 (1954): 255-57.

Smith, E. Gene. "The New Delhi Office of the Library of Congress at twenty: Changing acquisition parameters." *Library Acquisitions: Practice and Theory*. 6 (1982): 161-66.

Sohan Singh. "Books Program of the Asia Foundation in India." *Timeless Fellowship*. 2 (1965): 61-64.

Stevens, Robert D. "The Library of Congress Public Law 480 Programs." *Library Resources and Technical Services*. 7 (1963): 176-88.

Stieg, L. F. "American librarians abroad, 1946-65." *Library Quarterly*. 38 (1968): 315-22.

Suzuki, Yukihisa. *American Influence on the Development of Library Services in Japan, 1860-1941*. (Ph. D. Dissertation, University of Michigan. 1974.) *Dissertation Abstracts International*. 35 (1975): 7335A-7336A.

Swank, Raynard C. "Six items for export: International values in American librarianship." *Library Journal*. 88 (1963): 711-17.

Tripathi, V. "The story of Literacy House." *Indian Journal of Adult Education*. 40 (September 1979): 37-40.

Umapathy Setty, K. "Education for librarianship in India." *International Library Review*. 9 (1977): 289-301.

"USIA plans campaign to extend the role of American books." *Library of Congress Information Bulletin*. 44 (1985): 37-38.

Vann, Sarah K. "Dewey abroad: The field survey of 1964." *Library Resources and Technical Services*. 11(1967): 61-71.

Venkatesan, P. "Dr. S. R. Ranganathan–The World Librarian and Father of Indian library movement–A chronology." *RILISAR Bulletin*. 1 (1983): 43-52.

Vickery, B. C. Review of "Prolegomena to library classification: 2nd ed. 1957. *Library Quarterly*. 28 (1958): 219-20.

Viswanathan, C. G. "A hundred years of Indian university libraries, 1857-1956." *Library Association Record*. 59 (1957): 393-96.

Vosper, Robert G. "A century abroad." *College and Research Libraries*. 37 (1976): 514-30.

Vyas, S. D. "American Studies Research Centre Library." *Library Herald*. 20 (1981-82): 139-50.

Wessells, Helen E. "International cooperation." *Library Trends*. 3 (1954-55): 308-18.

Winger, Howard. W., Ed. "American library history: 1876-1976." *Library Trends*. 25 (1976-77): 1-416.

—. "Aspects of librarianship: a trace work of history." *Library Quarterly*. 31 (1961): 321-35.

ANNUAL REPORTS

India Government, Ministry of Education. *Annual Report*, 1955-56, 1957-58, 1958-59.

Indian Institute of Technology, Kanpur. *Annual Report,* 1961-62, 1962-63, 1968-69.

Library of Congress. *Annual Report of the Librarian* for the fiscal year ending June 30, 1961, 1965, 1967, 1969, 1970, 1978, and for the fiscal year ending September 30, 1980, 1981, 1983, 1984.

National Institute of Virology (Virus Research Centre), Pune. *Annual Report*, 1954-55, 1958-59 to 1974-75.

National Library, Calcutta. *Annual Report*, 1955-56.

Punjab University, Chandigarh. *Annual Report*, 1960 to 1964

Rockefeller Foundation, New York. Annual Report, 1954, 1955, 1957, to 1963, 1965, 1966.

LETTERS

American Studies Research Centre, Hyderabad. 29 September 1983.

Asheim, Lester. 30 March 1984.

Asia Foundation, San Francisco. 5 August 1983, 24 September 1984.

Bhatia, Kanta, Philadelphia. 11 June 1985.

Bourne, Charles P. 17 May 1984.

Calcutta University. 2 May 1984.

Carnegie Corporation, New York. 18 September 1985.

Central Leather Research Institute, Madras. 25 January 1984.

College of Engineering, Guindy. 26 September 1984.

deBenko, Eugene. 1 April 1985, 2 August 1985.

Deccan College Post-graduate and Research Institute, Pune. 26 September 1984.

Dhyani, Pushpa, Jaipur, 21 January 1984.

Ford Foundation Office, New Delhi. 21 May 1984.

G. B. Pant Social Science Institute, Allahabad. 17 October 1985.

Holt, Beatrice H. to K. S. Deshpande. 21 February 1961.

India International Centre, New Delhi. 18 August 1983.

International Crop Research Institute for Semi-Arid Tropic (ICRISAT), Hyderabad. 24 July 1984.

Kharbas, Datta S., Rochester. 17 May 1985.

Kumar, P. S. G., Nagpur. 25 July 1984.

Lancaster, F. W. 27 September 1984.

Metcalf, Keyes D. to B. S. Kesavan. 19 March, 1959.
—— to the Rockefeller Foundation (from New Delhi). 19 March 1959.
Nagar, Murari Lal, Missouri-Columbia. 27 March 1985.
Penland, Patrick R. 28 March 1984.
Perreault, Jean M. 26 March 1984.
Rogers, A. Robert. 25 October 1983.
Scholberg, Henry. 20 March 1984.
Smith, E. Gene. 15 August 1985.
Unesco, Paris. 4 May 1984.
Wasserman, Paul. 1 May 1984.
White, Carl M. to H. C. Mehta. 15 February 1967 and 28 August 1972.

INTERVIEWS

Bhattacharyya, Ganesh. Bangalore, 29 November 1983.
Chapman, Ronald. Hyderabad, 5 September 1985.
Chaudhuri, Shubha. New Delhi, 17 May 1985.
Dasgupta, Kalpana. Calcutta, 24 May 1984.
Deshpande, K. S. Dharwad, 28 June 1984.
Garde, P. K. Pune, 18 September 1985.
Issac, K. A. Pune, 18 October 1984.
Kaula, P. N. Pune, 17 January 1984.
Shetge, M. S. Bombay, 21 December 1983.
Srivastava, A. P. Delhi, 2 May 1985.
Srivastava, V. P. Lucknow, 10 May 1985.
Thiagarajan, R. New Delhi, 26 April 1985.
Thiruvengadam, R. Madras, 25 November 1983.

INDEX